Essential Legal English in Context

Essential Legal English in Context

Understanding the Vocabulary of
US Law and Government

Karen M. Ross

New York University Press

New York

NEW YORK UNIVERSITY PRESS
New York
www.nyupress.org

References to Internet websites (URLs) were accurate at the time of writing.
Neither the author nor New York University Press is responsible for URLs
that may have expired or changed since the manuscript was prepared.

Library of Congress Cataloging-in-Publication Data
Names: Ross, Karen M., author.
Title: Essential legal English in context : understanding the vocabulary of
U.S. law and government / Karen M. Ross.
Description: New York : New York University Press, 2019. |
Also available as an ebook. | Includes bibliographical references and index.
Identifiers: LCCN 2018043754| ISBN 9781479854806 (cl : alk. paper) |
ISBN 1479854808 (cl : alk. paper) | ISBN 9781479831678 (pb : alk. paper) |
ISBN 1479831670 (pb : alk. paper)
Subjects: LCSH: Law—United States—Terminology. | Law—United
States—Language. | English language—Usage. | United States—Politics
and government—Outlines, syllabi, etc. | Law—United States—Outlines,
syllabi, etc.
Classification: LCC KF156 .R67 2019 | DDC 340/.014—dc23
LC record available at https://lccn.loc.gov/2018043754

New York University Press books are printed on acid-free paper,
and their binding materials are chosen for strength and durability.
We strive to use environmentally responsible suppliers and materials
to the greatest extent possible in publishing our books.

Manufactured in the United States of America

10 9 8 7 6 5 4 3 2 1

Also available as an ebook

I dedicate this book to my wonderful family:
my husband, Michael;
our children, Brian, Katie, and Matthew;
my parents, Herbert and Enid Morrison;
and my brother, Ken Morrison, and family.

Contents

Preface

What are the similarities or differences between

- taking *the* stand and taking *a* stand?
- a bill, a statute, legislation, a law, and an act?
- a level of government and a branch of government?
- a top court, a high court, a federal court of last resort, and a state court of last resort?
- treaties and treatises?

What are

- partisanship, bipartisanship, and nonpartisanship?
- political gridlock?
- transparency?
- decisions on the merits?

Essential Legal English in Context answers these and many other questions while introducing the US legal system and its terminology. Designed especially for international lawyers and students who are not familiar with the US legal system and its vocabulary, *Essential Legal English in Context* illustrates how legal language relates to the structure of the US government.

This book provides a valuable self-study tool to use before entering a US law school, studying US law or government, or working as a seconded attorney to a US law firm and has the following goals:

- To explain basic concepts related to federal, state, and local levels and branches of government
- To define law-related vocabulary in the context of the US Constitution and the legislative, executive, and judicial branches of government
- To prepare to read US judicial decisions by unpacking concepts embedded in these decisions, such as the sources that courts interpret—constitutional provisions, statutes from the legislature, executive orders from the executive, and common law rules from the judiciary
- To introduce selected current political issues and legal topics, including an overview of how the lawmaking process works in today's US society
- To illustrate how the US constitutional separation of powers and checks and balances come into play when courts interpret the law

Throughout the book there are

- *Exercises*, which allow readers to apply and extend their knowledge
- *Word studies*, which explain similarities and differences in related, or similarly spelled, legal terminology and concepts
- *Research updates*, which signal certain areas to research in order to determine the current status of that subject area.

This book is aimed at providing general information to international lawyers and students, newly admitted law students, and others who are unfamiliar with the US legal system and its vocabulary. It is not intended to give legal advice or to address with specificity any legal issue or legal topic. Rather, it is intended to provide a broad overview of questions that are likely to be encountered by those who are new to the US legal system. Readers should keep in mind that many concepts have been admittedly oversimplified and the legal terms and institutions discussed in this book have been distilled in order to provide a simple and basic understanding of legal vocabulary. The definition of legal terms in the United States often varies significantly from jurisdiction to jurisdiction. In addition, the terminology included in the book may have other meanings in different contexts. For ease of understanding, this book describes legal terminology in what the author believes is the most commonly understood context.

Acknowledgments

I thank Dr. Frank Tang of the New York University Steinhardt School for making the classroom an inspiring place and for sharing his teaching gifts. Thank you to my exceptional colleagues at New York University School of Law, Mary Holland, Director of the Graduate Lawyering Program, for her leadership, and Irene Segal Ayers, Deputy Director of the Graduate Lawyering Program, for generously sharing her valuable input. I also thank Jerry Snider for his beneficial advice and support.

In addition, I am grateful to Andrew Katz for his insight and outstanding design, and Clara Platter and Martin Coleman at NYU Press for their vision and assistance.

I acknowledge all of my international LLM students for their exceptional dedication and their questions, which inspired this book: they have all made my teaching most worthwhile.

UNIT 1 Overview of the Government in the United States

The Three Levels of Government

The Type of Government That Exists in the United States

The United States has a *federal* system of government. In this system, both federal and separate state governments have certain powers to regulate behavior and create an ordered society. State governments within each individual state grant certain powers to local governments (such as cities).[1]

Federal describes this system of government and is also a term referring to the one central government that creates rules governing behavior in all of the fifty states.

The Three Levels of Government in the United States

Federal Level

One central government creating rules that generally govern behavior throughout the United States, including every state and local area in the United States.

State Level

Fifty individual governments (one in each of the fifty states) creating rules that generally govern behavior in that one state. Different states can have different laws on the same subject. State laws are distinct from federal laws.

Local Level

Numerous individual governments of smaller geographic units within each state, including counties and municipalities (cities, villages, and towns), create rules that generally govern behavior in that one local geographic unit.

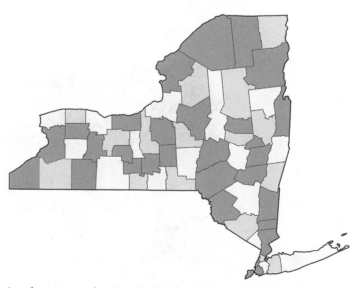

Local counties within New York State

EXERCISE 1 | **The Levels of Government**

Instructions: Review "The Three Levels of Government" in lesson 1.1. Then decide whether the following statements are true or false and circle your selection.

1. People in both the states of California and Missouri must all comply with federal laws. **True** **False**

2. People in California (while in California) must comply with both California state laws and Missouri state laws. **True** **False**

3. People in the city of Phoenix in the state of Arizona (while in Phoenix) must abide by at least three sets of laws: federal laws, Arizona state laws, and local Phoenix laws. **True** **False**

4. People in the city of Tallahassee in the state of Florida (while in Tallahassee) must abide by federal laws, laws of the state of Georgia, and laws of the city of Tallahassee. **True** **False**

The Types of Laws That Each of These Three Levels of Government Create

In the United States' federal system, each of the three government levels—the federal level, the state level, and the local level—create different types of laws.

Federal Level: One Federal Government

Federal laws generally govern behavior throughout every state and local area in the United States, and there is one set of federal laws. This same federal law applies regardless of whether a person is in Hawaii, California, New York, or any of the other states or localities.

The following are examples of federal laws that can be enforced in every state.

▸ Federal crimes: Crimes prosecuted in federal courts include
  ▪ arson (setting a fire) of a federal building such as an office building owned by the federal government; and
  ▪ assault of a federal employee (such as an FBI agent).
▸ Federal taxes: Every United States citizen with certain income (earnings) must pay taxes to the federal government, as required by the federal tax laws.

- ► Federal regulations: Federal agencies create uniform rules that apply throughout the United States, such as
  - air safety for airplanes (Federal Aviation Administration);
  - food labeling and safety of new drugs (Food and Drug Administration); and
  - health care (Department of Health and Human Services).

State Level: Fifty State Governments

State laws govern behavior in individual states, such as New York, California, and Florida. In contrast to the one uniform set of federal laws, each individual state has its own laws that are distinct from the other forty-nine states.

The following are examples of state laws that are enforced within one state.

- ► State crimes: Crimes defined by the different state legislatures are prosecuted in state courts (and not federal courts), including
  - arson of a privately owned home used solely for a person's residence; and
  - assault of a state police officer or another person who is in that state.
- ► State taxes: Different states have different laws governing payment of state taxes. New York and California require that residents with certain income pay tax to the state on their income (money that they earn), as state tax laws prescribe. In Florida, residents do not have to pay state taxes on their income, but they do have to pay sales taxes and like all other citizens, when required, must pay federal taxes. Many people, including retirees, move to Florida for its favorable tax laws (and warm weather). Each state has its own distinct tax laws.

Local Level: Numerous Local Governments within Each Individual State

Local laws primarily affect people within that local area, such as a city like New York City or Los Angeles. However, the types of laws that local governments can create are limited because state governments have the power to create many laws that apply throughout the state. *Home rule* defines the scope of certain local governments' powers to create local laws.[2]

The following are examples of local laws that may only be enforced within a certain local area:

- ► Building codes.
- ► Parking rules on city or other local streets.
- ► Local taxes: Residents and businesses in local communities pay taxes such as property taxes on houses or buildings that they own. They also pay county, municipal, or other taxes to pay for important services close to their homes, such as funding local police departments, fire departments, and building departments and school taxes to fund public schools for the education of children living in the local community.

EXERCISE 2 | Governments' Powers to Create Law

Background: Each level of government governs, and controls behavior, primarily within its own borders. One goal of federal law is to create uniform (one identical) set of rules that apply equally in every state, regardless of the state's location, such as rules to promote safe air travel. The rules governing which level of government has the power to create specific laws will be reviewed in later lessons. For now, consider which level of government should govern specific conduct within its borders.

Instructions: Read the description of specific laws listed in column 1. If you decide that one central *federal* government should govern this behavior uniformly throughout the United States, write *federal* in column 2. If a smaller *state* or *local* government, whose residents may have different needs, should regulate the activity, then write *state* or *local* in column 2. You may insert more than one possible answer for each law.

Column 1 *Law*	Column 2 *Insert "federal," "state," or "local" in the blank*
1. The transportation of stolen cars from one state to another, in interstate commerce	
2. Car theft, without the transportation of that vehicle from one state to another	
3. Parking rules on streets	S
4. Tax laws	F / S
5. Possession of a gun within 1,000 feet of a school	S
6. Immigration laws, governing when a person can enter the United States	F
7. Protecting a person or entity's scientific inventions from copying by others	F
8. The purchase of health insurance by every US citizen	f
9. Allowing a person to recover money for injuries suffered as a bystander after observing the death of one's dog	S
10. Criminalizing the theft of secret scientific materials	
11. Allowing dogs to sit with an owner in a restaurant's outdoor seating area while the dog owner is dining	L
12. Covenants not to compete, which are contract provisions restricting a person from competing with a former employer or a person to whom one's business is sold	S

WORD STUDY | *Federal, the Feds, the Fed*

Similarly spelled words can have different meanings, such as the following words that all begin with *fed*:

Federal refers to one central government governing the behavior of all people within the United States.

The feds is a colloquial expression describing various members of the federal government including Federal Bureau of Investigation (FBI) law enforcement agents; Immigration and Customs Enforcement (ICE) agents, who find people living illegally within the United States; or United States attorneys, who represent the United States government in federal civil and criminal court cases.

The Fed refers, specifically, to the Federal Reserve, encompassing the central bank of the United States.

The federal government	The feds	The Fed
Three branches: **1.** Legislature **2.** Executive **3.** Judiciary		
	The feds include FBI law enforcement agents and others. The FBI investigates federal crimes such as terrorism, cyber crime, and organized crime.	The Fed is the Federal Reserve Bank.

EXERCISE 3 | Word Fill-In

Instructions: Fill in the blanks with the correct words from the word box. You may use a word more than once.

Word Box				
federal	feds	state	local	Fed

The United States has a _____ system of government in which power is shared between a central government and the state governments. Three levels of government exist on the _federal_ , _state_ and _local_ levels. Governments can create laws that protect people from harm, such as laws defining crimes. They can also create laws that restrict behavior, such as texting while driving, or laws that mandate (require) specific behavior, such as paying taxes.

The federal government has one uniform set of laws and can create _federal_ laws affecting people throughout the United States equally. By contrast, _state_ and _local_ governments may have different needs and powers requiring different sets of laws that protect people within their borders. For example, states in the North with severely cold weather must have money to fund trucks, salt, and other equipment to clear snow from the roads during the winter, while states in the South must have resources to clean up following other kinds of severe weather such as hurricanes.

Members of the federal government, such as the FBI and other federal law enforcement agents, may be referred to as the _feds_ : they protect citizens by investigating crimes. A different arm of the federal government, known as the _Fed_ , is the central bank of the United States, making monetary policy, such as deciding an important interest rate.

The Founding Documents

The Federal Constitution, State Constitutions, and Local Charters

The Founding Documents of the Federal, State, and Local Governments

Federal Constitution

Founding documents set forth basic rules governing the levels of the United States government and give these governments specific powers to create rules governing behavior, and the federal and state constitutions guarantee certain individual rights.

Founding Document of the Federal Government

The Federal Constitution set up the federal government in the United States over 200 years ago.

THE CONSTITUTION OF
THE
STATE OF NEW YORK

As Revised, with Amendments adopted
by the Constitutional Convention of 1938
and Approved by Vote of the People on
November 8, 1938
and
Amendments subsequently adopted by the
Legislature and Approved by Vote of the People.

As Amended and in Force January 1, 2015

ARTICLE I
BILL OF RIGHTS

§1. Rights, privileges and franchise secured;
power of legislature to dispense with primary
elections in certain cases.
2. Trial by jury; how waived.
3. Freedom of worship; religious liberty.
4. Habeas corpus.
5. Bail; fines; punishments; detention of
witnesses.
6. Grand jury; protection of certain
enumerated rights; duty of public officers to
sign waiver of immunity and give testimony;
penalty for refusal.
7. Compensation for taking private property;
private roads; drainage of agricultural lands.
8. Freedom of speech and press; criminal
prosecutions for libel.
9. Right to assemble and petition; divorce;
lotteries; pool-selling and gambling; laws to
prevent; pari-mutuel betting on horse races
permitted; games of chance, bingo or lotto
authorized under certain restrictions.
10. [Repealed.]
11. Equal protection of laws; discrimination in
civil rights prohibited.
12. Security against unreasonable searches,
seizures and interceptions.
13. [Repealed.]
14. Common law and acts of the colonial and
state legislatures.
15. [Repealed.]
16. Damages for injuries causing death.
17. Labor not a commodity; hours and wages in
public work; right to organize and bargain
collectively.
18. Workers' compensation. . . .

ARTICLE III
LEGISLATURE

§1. Legislative power.
2. Number and terms of senators and
assemblymen.
3. Senate districts.
4. Readjustments and reapportionments; when
federal census to control.
5. Apportionment of assemblymen; creation of
assembly districts.
5-a. Definition of inhabitants.
5-b. Independent redistricting commission.
6. Compensation, allowances and traveling
expenses of members.
7. Qualifications of members; prohibitions on
certain civil appointments; acceptance to
vacate seat.
8. Time of elections of members.
9. Powers of each house.
10. Journals; open sessions; adjournments.
11. Members not to be questioned for speeches.
12. Bills may originate in either house; may be
amended by the other
13. Enacting clause of bills; no law to be enacted
except by bill.
14. Manner of passing bills; message of necessity
for immediate vote.
15. Private or local bills to embrace only one
subject, expressed in title.
16. Existing law not to be made applicable by
reference.
17. Cases in which private or local bills shall not
be passed.
18. Extraordinary sessions of the legislature;
power to convene on legislative initiative.
19. Private claims not to be audited by
legislature; claims barred by lapse of time.
20. Two-thirds bills.
21. Certain sections not to apply to bills
recommended by certain commissioners or
public agencies.
22. Tax laws to state tax and object distinctly;
definition of income for income tax purposes
by reference to federal laws authorized.
23. When yeas and nays necessary; three-fifths
to constitute quorum.
24. Prison labor; contract system abolished.
25. Emergency governmental operations;
legislature to provide for.

ARTICLE IV
EXECUTIVE

§1. Executive power; election and terms of
governor and lieutenant- governor.
2. Qualifications of governor and lieutenant-
governor.
3. Powers and duties of governor;
compensation.
4. Reprieves, commutations and pardons;
powers and duties of governor relating to
grants of.
5. When lieutenant-governor to act as
governor.
6. Duties and compensation of lieutenant-
governor; succession to the governorship.
7. Action by governor on legislative bills;
reconsideration after veto.
8. Departmental rules and regulations; filing;
publication.

ARTICLE VI
JUDICIARY

§1. Unified court system; organization; process.
2. Court of appeals; organization; designations;
vacancies, how filled; commission on judicial
nomination.
3. Court of appeals; jurisdiction.
4. Judicial departments; appellate divisions,
how constituted; governor to designate
justices; temporary assignments;
jurisdiction.
5. Appeals from judgment or order; new trial.
6. Judicial districts; how constituted; supreme
court.
7. Supreme court; jurisdiction.
8. Appellate terms; composition; jurisdiction.
9. Court of claims; jurisdiction.
10. County courts; judges.
11. County court; jurisdiction.
12. Surrogate's courts; judges; jurisdiction.
13. Family court; organization; jurisdiction.
14. Discharge of duties of more than one judicial
office by same judicial officer.
15. New York city; city-wide courts; jurisdiction.
16. District courts; jurisdiction; judges.
17. Town, village and city courts; jurisdiction;
judges.
18. Trial by jury; trial without jury; claims
against state.
19. Transfer of actions and proceedings.
20. Judges and justices; qualifications; eligibility
for other office or service; restrictions.
21. Vacancies; how filled.
22. Commission on judicial conduct;
composition; organization and procedure;
review by court of appeals; discipline of
judges or justices.

Founding Documents of State Governments

State constitutions set up each of the fifty state governments. For example, the New York State Constitution establishes the basic rules for New York state government; the California Constitution establishes the basic rules for California state government; the Texas Constitution establishes the basic rules for the Texas state government. Every state has its own constitution.

Founding Documents of Local Governments

Within each state, the smaller geographic units such as counties and municipalities (cities and others) may have local founding documents. As one example, the New York City Charter sets forth certain rules governing the New York City government.

CITY OF NEW YORK
CITY CHARTER
CONTENTS
(As amended by local laws 1-72
and chapters 1, 4-698
of 2003)

How Many Constitutions Exist in the United States?

There are at least fifty-one constitutions in the United States:

- ► There is one Federal Constitution.
- ► There are fifty state constitutions—one for each of the fifty states.
- ► Other areas, called *territories* and *commonwealths*, are part of the United States and may or may not have a constitution: for example, Guam does not have a constitution, but Puerto Rico does.

There are also numerous documents governing individual local governments that may have different names, such as a *charter*.

Why Is It Important to Distinguish Federal, State, and Local Founding Documents?

Certain founding documents define the types of laws that governments can implement. That is, certain levels and branches of government have the power to create laws as outlined in the founding documents.

When a specific branch of government creates a law that may exceed the powers granted to it by a founding document, a person or entity (such as a business) affected by that law could bring a lawsuit against the government, claiming that the law is unconstitutional (inconsistent with the constitution's specific grant of power). As an example, during former president Barack Obama's administration, a business organization and others sued the federal government claiming that a new federal law creating sweeping changes to health care in the United States was unconstitutional. They asserted that the Federal Constitution did not give the federal legislature the power to enact this health care law.

Later lessons address the constitutional powers of the branches of government as outlined in founding documents, including

- ► What kinds of laws can each level of government enact?
- ► What constitutional powers do the branches of government have?

WORD STUDY | *Word Forms*

By identifying a word's part of speech, such as whether the word is a noun, verb, adjective, or adverb, one can begin to form grammatical sentences.

The basic sentence structure in English is subject, verb, and object. Adjectives modify nouns, and adverbs modify verbs and certain other parts of speech.

Subject (noun)	Verb	Adjective	Object (noun)
The United States Constitution	created the	federal	government.

Term	Part of speech (noun, verb, adjective, adverb)	Meaning
Constitu*tion* -*ion*, noun ending	Noun	Founding document of the federal and state governments
To constitute	Verb (base form)	To make up, as in parts making up a whole
Constitution*al* -*al*, adjective ending	Adjective	Relating to the constitution
Constitutional*ly* -*ly*, adverb ending	Adverb	Consistent with a constitution

EXERCISE 4 | Word Forms

Instructions: Choose one of the word forms from the chart above to fill in the blanks, and then explain why you chose that word form. You may use a word more than once. The first sentence is completed as a model.

1. *Constitutional* amendments of the US Constitution must be passed by two-thirds of the states.
   Constitutional is an adjective modifying the noun *amendments*. *Amendments* is the subject-noun of this sentence.

2. The Congress, the president, and other members of the federal executive and judicial branches _____ the federal government.

3. The Federal _____ establishes the basic rules for the federal government.

4. A_____ government is a government in which the powers of the government are set out in a constitution.

5. Each of the fifty states has a state _____.

6. The United States Supreme Court decided if Congress acted _____ when creating a new health care law.

7. The fifty states, together, _____ the United States.

EXERCISE 5 | Questions

1. What are *founding documents*, and which *founding documents* set forth the basic rules governing the federal, state, and local governments?

2. How many constitutions exist in the United States?

3. Why is it important to distinguish between federal, state, and local founding documents?

LESSON 1.3 The Three Branches of United States Government

Differentiating *Levels* of Government from *Branches* of Government

A *level* of government refers to either a federal, state, or local government. By comparison, a *branch* of government refers to the three governing units *within* each level of government: a legislature, an executive, and a judiciary.

Certain founding documents grant and allocate powers to each level of government. To allocate powers means to distribute and assign powers to the three distinct branches of government on each level.

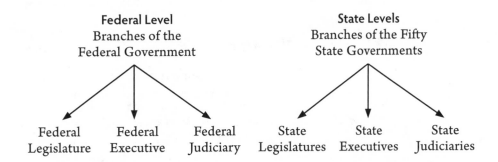

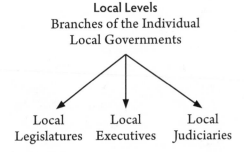

The Three Branches of the Federal, State, and Local Governments

Federal Level: The Branches of the Federal Government

Since there is only one federal government for all of the United States, there is only

1. one federal legislative branch, called Congress, which consists of the Senate and the House of Representatives;
2. one federal executive branch, which consists of the president, the vice president, the Cabinet, and other federal administrative agencies; and
3. one federal judicial branch, which includes an entire system of federal courts.*

* There is only one United States Supreme Court, located in Washington, DC. Other federal courts are located throughout United States.

State Level: The Branches of the Fifty State Governments

Each state has its own system of government consisting of three branches of state government. There are therefore (at least) 150 branches of state government throughout the United States, including

1. fifty distinct state legislatures, which enact state laws—in New York, for example, the state legislature consists of two Houses: the Senate and the Assembly;
2. fifty distinct state executives, which include the governor and lieutenant governor and state administrative agencies in each state; and
3. fifty distinct state judiciaries, which consist of an entire system of state courts.

Local Level: The Branches of the Local Governments within Each State

Within each state, there are numerous local county and municipal (city) or other governments, which may have three branches, including the following:

1. Local legislatures, which may enact local laws.[3] For instance, in New York City, the local legislature is called the City Council, and in certain geographic units called counties, the legislature is called a county legislature.
2. Local executives, which include the mayor or the local executive of certain counties, and local regulatory agencies. One example of a local regulatory agency is the New York City Department of Buildings, which investigates building construction violations in New York City.

** Review Article VI of the New York State Constitution in lesson 1.2, to see New York court names.

3. Local courts, which are set up differently within each state. In New York, the state constitution and state statutes specify how both state and local courts are set up.** Local courts hear specific types of local cases, and there are certain courts hearing cases in local counties, such as a family court, a county court, a surrogate's court, and a civil court.

WORD STUDY | *Primary Authority*

Primary authorities are sources of law from one of the branches of government. The following chart is a comparison of portions of the federal and the New York State constitutions and the primary authorities from these two levels of government. Local governments also create local laws that are primary authority.

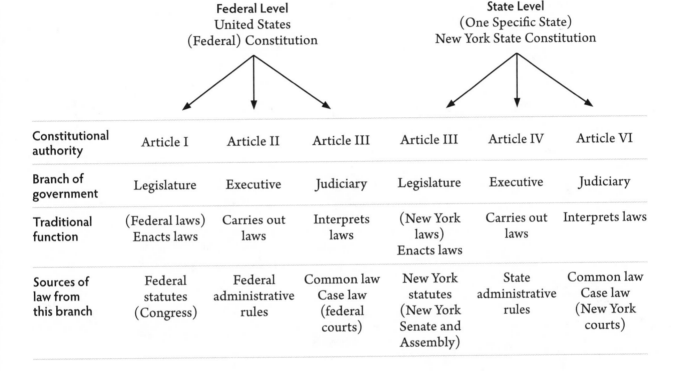

	Federal Level United States (Federal) Constitution			State Level (One Specific State) New York State Constitution		
Constitutional authority	Article I	Article II	Article III	Article III	Article IV	Article VI
Branch of government	Legislature	Executive	Judiciary	Legislature	Executive	Judiciary
Traditional function	(Federal laws) Enacts laws	Carries out laws	Interprets laws	(New York laws) Enacts laws	Carries out laws	Interprets laws
Sources of law from this branch	Federal statutes (Congress)	Federal administrative rules	Common law Case law (federal courts)	New York statutes (New York Senate and Assembly)	State administrative rules	Common law Case law (New York courts)

EXERCISE 6 | Questions

1. What is the difference between a *level* of government and a *branch* of government?

2. What are the three branches of the United States government on each of the following levels? What is the name of the founding document setting up these branches of government on these separate levels? Fill in the answers to these questions on the following page.

Branches of government on the federal level:

a.

b.

c.

Founding document:

Branches of government on the state levels:

a.

b.

c.

Founding documents for each state:

Branches of government on the local levels:

a.

b.

c.

Founding documents for certain local counties and cities:

LESSON 1.4 The Federal Constitution

Historical Background and the Separation of Powers

The United States gained freedom from England in the late 1700s. When setting up the United States' new government, the Constitution's writers (called the *Founding Fathers*, *founders*, or *framers* of the Constitution) feared the creation of an overly powerful central government, like the former governing monarchy led by the king of England. It was therefore important for the framers to create a document that would balance the need to create this strong central government to protect the nation as a whole with the need to preserve state powers and individual freedoms of the people.

Two other important goals of the Founding Fathers were to unify the separate states with one central government and to separate the powers among the three branches so that no single branch was overly powerful. To do so, the Founding Fathers balanced powers among the three branches of government, giving each branch of government different functions:

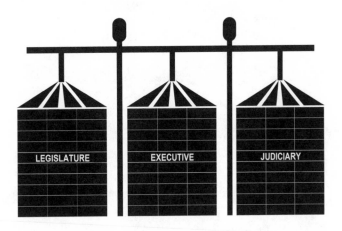

The separation of powers, in theory, keeps each branch of government in line.
Checks and balances: Each branch has the power to oversee, or *check*, the powers of the other branches so that no single branch of government becomes too powerful.

Overview of the Federal Constitution and Federal Constitutional Excerpts

* *Vest* means to give authority or power to act.

The Federal Constitution begins with a "Preamble" listing the framers' goals in setting up the federal government and contains separate *articles*, that vest* specific powers in the branches of the federal government:

Preamble

We the People of the United States, in Order to form a more perfect Union, establish Justice, insure domestic Tranquility, provide for the common defence,** promote the general Welfare, and secure the Blessings of Liberty to ourselves and our Posterity [future generations], do ordain and establish this Constitution for the United States of America.

** *Defence* is the British spelling of the word, and *defense* is the US spelling.

Article I, Section 1. *The federal legislature* (Congress)
All legislative Powers herein granted shall be vested in a Congress of the United States, which shall consist of a Senate and House of Representatives.

Article II, Section 1. *The federal executive* (The president, vice president, Cabinet, Department of Justice, and other administrative agencies)
The executive Power shall be vested in a President of the United States of America. He shall hold his Office during the Term of four Years . . . together with the Vice President, chosen for the same Term.

Article III, Section 1. *The federal judiciary* (The United States Supreme Court and inferior [lower] federal courts)
The judicial Power of the United States shall be vested in one supreme Court, and in such inferior Courts as the Congress may from time to time ordain and establish.

EXERCISE 7 | Words in Context

1. Under the Federal Constitution, what types of powers are *vested* in

   a. the legislature?

   b. the executive?

   c. the judiciary?

2. Read the constitutional excerpts on the previous page, and then answer the following questions:

   a. What is another name for the federal legislature?

   b. What does Congress consist of?

   c. What does the federal executive consist of?

   d. What does the federal judiciary consist of?

   e. Which branch of government creates the federal courts (other than the United States Supreme Court)?

The Preamble to the Federal Constitution

Pre- is a prefix meaning "before."

The Preamble*—the first fifty-two words of the Federal Constitution—comes before the primary articles of the Constitution and begins with the following words:

We the People of the United States . . .

The words "We the people" were written in a larger size to highlight that this Constitution is for the benefit of the people, rather than members of government, like the overly powerful monarch and British government from which the first Americans gained their freedom. As stated by one source, this larger size reinforces a founding principle:

affirm[ing] that the government of the United States exists to serve its citizens.[4]

EXERCISE 8 | Preamble

Instructions: Review the Preamble, and then answer the following questions:

1. What goals of the federal government are listed in the Preamble?

2. What does *posterity* mean?

WORD STUDY | *United States, Federal, and National*

United States and *federal* can be synonyms, referring to the federal government. *United States* can refer to the country, as in the following context: "Voters in the United States elect representatives on the federal, state, and local levels." In other contexts, *United States* can function as an adjective meaning "federal": The *United States Constitution* is also called the *Federal Constitution* setting up the one central government. Similarly, a *United States* court can mean a court in the *federal* system, as compared to a state or local court, and a *United States* judge can mean a judge sitting in a *federal* system, as compared to a judge sitting in a state or local court, depending on the context.

The *United States* District Court for the District of Alaska is a federal trial court located in the state of Alaska. By contrast, the Nassau *County* District Court in New York is a local court within a local geographic area called a county.

National is an adjective referring to a particular nation or country.*

* The terms *United States* and *national* may refer specifically to a part of the *federal*, as opposed to a state or local, government.

The Thurgood Marshall *United States* Courthouse in lower Manhattan, where *United States* (*federal*) judges hear certain *federal* cases. It is named for the former United States Supreme Court justice Thurgood Marshall.

EXERCISE 9 | Word Fill-In

Instructions: Fill in the blanks with the correct words from the word box. You may use a term more than once.

Word Box		
Founding Fathers, founders, framers	federal	feds
national	United States	Fed

1. Congress enacted the US Patriot Act to protect _____ security interests.

2. The _____ government consists of three branches: Congress; the president, the vice president, the Cabinet, and administrative agencies; and the federal courts.

3. _____ statutes from Congress are printed in the _____ Code.

4. The _____ investigate potential violations of _____ law.

5. The _____ wanted to ensure that the _____ government had the power to effectively protect the entire nation, while preserving important states' and individuals' rights.

6. Several economists questioned the decision of the _____ to temporarily maintain low interest rates.

WORD STUDY | *Law*

Law has both a general meaning and a specific meaning depending on the context.

▸ In one general meaning, *law* means the collective body of rules from a constitution and created by the three branches of government.

▸ In a specific meaning, *law* means only one specific type of rule: a *constitutional provision or amendment* in a constitution; *statutes* from the legislatures; *administrative rules and regulations* from the administrative agencies; and *common law rules and precedent* from the judiciary.

We may use the word *law* even when referring only to a specific rule from a single branch of government, and it is therefore important to understand if the context refers to the general or the specific meaning.

General meaning in context: "*Law* exists to create an ordered society." Here, *law* has a general meaning of rules from a constitution and created by the three branches of government.

Specific meanings in context:

► Congress passed a new health care *law*.

Here, *law* has a specific meaning of a federal statute from the federal (and not a state) legislature.

► The Federal Aviation Administration promulgated *laws* regulating drone use.

Here *law* has a specific meaning of administrative rules from a federal agency.

► The *law* is clear: a person who is interrogated by the police officers while in custody must be given *Miranda* warnings.

Here, *law* also has a specific meaning of a rule originally from the judiciary, the United States Supreme Court, created in a court case called *Miranda v. Arizona*, 384 U.S. 436 (1966).

When judges issue written opinions during one particular case, they are interpreting one or more specific types of law. This "law" may come from a constitution or any one or more of the branches of government (legislature, executive, or judiciary) on any one or more levels of government (federal, state, or local) and others not covered in this book, such as certain international sources. Unit 5 gives examples of how courts have interpreted specific sources of law.

Understanding specific details about each branch of government will give context to explain legal terms. The next units examine each branch of government individually, reviewing the

► constitutional authority creating that branch of government;
► structure;
► powers;
► source of law created; and
► vocabulary and terminology arising in the context of each branch of government.

Unit 1 Review

Instructions: For each of the following phrases, underline the word indicating that it relates to the federal government, a state government, or a local government, and then write which branch of government is described, if any. The first one is completed as a model.

1. A <u>United States</u> judge: federal judiciary (*United States* indicates federal, and *judge* describes a member of a judiciary)

2. The mayor of Chicago:

3. The United States Constitution:

4. The California Constitution:

5. The United States Court of Appeals:

6. The United States District Court:

7. The Nassau County District Court:

8. The Civil Court of the City of New York:

9. The governor of Iowa:

10. The feds:

11. The United States Code:

12. The New York Penal Law:

13. The national government:

14. The Supreme Court of the State of New York, Bronx County:

15. The United States Supreme Court:

UNIT 2   The Federal Legislature

LESSON 2.1 Constitutional Authority for the Federal Legislature

Article I, Section 1 of the United States Constitution vests federal legislative powers as follows:

> All legislative Powers herein granted shall be vested in a Congress of the United States, which shall consist of a Senate and House of Representatives.

The United States' legislative body, called *Congress*, is located on Capitol* Hill (The Hill) in Washington, DC.

Congress means only the two chambers of the *federal legislature*: the Senate and the House of Representatives. By contrast, the general term *legislature* may mean

* Capit*ol* (-*ol*) here refers to Congress, located on *Capitol Hill* in Washington, DC. Capit*al* (-*al*) is a city that is the main seat of a government. The capital of the United States is Washington, DC; the capital of Massachusetts is Boston. *Capital* can also refer to money, such as raising *capital*.

United States Capitol Building

any of the lawmaking bodies on either the federal, state, or local level. There is only one Congress (one federal legislature), but there are also fifty state legislatures and numerous local lawmaking bodies.

EXERCISE 10 | # Word Forms

Instructions: Define each of the following terms and write the word's part of speech, either noun, adjective, or verb. Then fill in the blanks in the following sentences with the correct term, making grammatical changes if necessary, such as adding a plural *s* or making the subject agree with the verb. You may use a word more than once.

Legislature:

Legislator:

Legislative:

To legislate:

Legislation:

Congress:

Congressperson:

Congressional:

1. _____ serve in Congress.

2. Congress _____ in order to create uniform rules applying within all of the fifty states.

3. A _____ is another name for a federal legislator. These elected representative serve in _____.

4. Article I vests _____ powers in the federal _____.

5. _____ history documents consist of records such as hearing transcripts and reports, detailing the reasons why _____ proposed _____.

6. A _____ report may be from the Senate or the House of Representatives.

LESSON 2.2 The Structure of the Federal Legislature

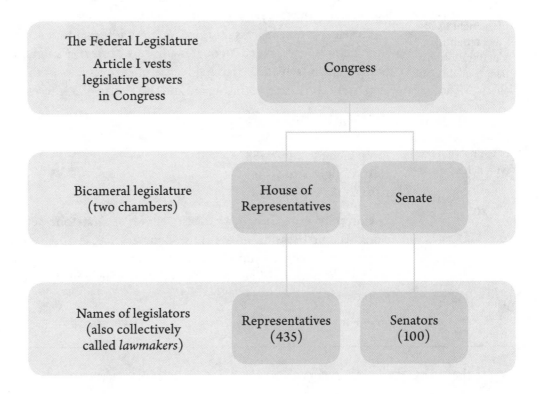

The Federal Legislature

Article I vests legislative powers in Congress

Congress

Bicameral legislature (two chambers)

House of Representatives

Senate

Names of legislators (also collectively called *lawmakers*)

Representatives (435)

Senators (100)

In the House of Representatives, there are a total of 435 representatives from all of the fifty states. The number of representatives from each state varies depending on that state's population and may change periodically according to a population count called a *census*. California, a state with a large population, has fifty-three representatives. States with smaller populations have fewer representatives, such as Rhode Island (two representatives) and Vermont (one representative).

By contrast, in the Senate, there are two senators from each state, for a total of one hundred senators, regardless of the state's population. California, Rhode Island, Vermont, and the other forty-seven states each have two senators.

WORD STUDY | *Legislator, Lawmakers, Constituent, Congress*

A *legislator* is a person who serves in a legislature, such as a senator in the Senate or a representative in the House of Representatives. In the states, legislators may have different names depending on the name of the body in which they serve. For example, in New York, the bicameral legislature consists of the Senate and Assembly, and the legislators who serve in the New York legislature are called New York senators (in the New York Senate) and New York assemblypersons (in the New York Assembly).

Citizens of every state vote in separate elections for their federal, state, and local legislators; another name for legislator is *lawmaker*. The people who vote* for the legislators are called *constituents*. Legislators represent their constituents in lawmaking bodies at the federal, state, and local levels of government.

The elected federal legislators in Congress vote on proposed laws during different time periods, each called a congress. In this context, *Congress* refers to the period of time during which the federal legislature enacts laws, rather than the bicameral legislature consisting of the Senate and the House of Representatives.

1st Congress: 1789–91
66th Congress: 1919–21
100th Congress: 1987–88
114th Congress: 2015–16
115th Congress: 2017–19

Currently, each Congress consists of two separate one-year periods, called sessions. The first session of the 114th Congress was in 2015, and the second session began in January 2016 and ended in December 2016.[1]

The job of federal *legislators* is to enact new federal laws during each session of Congress.

* *To disenfranchise* in this context means to deprive a person of the right to vote. Laws requiring identification that people might not be able to obtain, such as a driver's license, and stripping certain convicted criminals of voting rights disenfranchise voters.

Legislators in Congress

** The House of Representatives can be referred to as the *House*, with an upper-case *H*. By contrast, when referring to either house of Congress, in general terms and not by name, *house* has a lower-case *h*.

The following two sections of Article I specify the method of election, age, and citizenship requirements for legislators in each separate house of Congress.**

Article I, Section 2: The House of Representatives

The House of Representatives shall be composed of Members chosen every second Year by the People of the several States. . . .

No Person shall be a Representative who shall not have attained to the Age of twenty five Years, and been seven Years a Citizen of the United States, and who shall not, when elected, be an Inhabitant of that State in which he shall be chosen.

The floor of a congressional house

Article I, Section 3: The Senate
The Senate of the United States shall be composed of two Senators from each State
. . . [serving] for six Years. . . .

No person shall be a Senator who shall not have attained to the Age of thirty Years,
and been nine Years a Citizen of the United States, and who shall not, when elected,
be an Inhabitant of that State for which he shall be chosen.

EXERCISE 11 | Constitutional Excerpts

Instructions: Review the constitutional excerpts above, and then answer the following questions:

1. How often do constituents elect lawmakers to serve in the House (the House of
   Representatives)?

2. How often do constituents elect legislators to serve in the Senate?

3. How old do these elected officials have to be?

EXERCISE 12 | Congressional Terminology

Instructions: Match the terms in the left-hand column with the definitions in the right-hand column by writing the letter of the definition in front of the number of the term. The first one is completed as a model.

<u> i </u> **1.** Capitol Hill (The Hill)

_____ **2.** Capital

_____ **3.** Congress

_____ **4.** Congressional

_____ **5.** Senate

_____ **6.** US senators

_____ **7.** House of Representatives

_____ **8.** US representatives

_____ **9.** Constituents

a. This term has two meanings. It may mean both the House of Representatives and the Senate, collectively, or the time period during which federal legislators make laws.

b. The elected legislators who serve constituents in the House of Representatives.

c. A city in a particular state or the District of Columbia (DC) for the United States, which is the main seat of government.

d. Legislators represent these people, who live throughout the fifty states.

e. An adjective meaning "related to" Congress.

f. One of the two chambers of Congress.

g. The elected legislators who serve constituents in the US Senate.

h. One of the two chambers of Congress.

i. A description of the place where Congress is located in Washington, DC

WORD STUDY | *Idiom: Grilled on the Hill*

A synonym for intense questioning is *grilling*, from the verb *to grill*. A *grill* usually refers to a barbecue or cooking surface, which gives off intense heat. Being *grilled* has come to mean being asked questions in an intense way. When a person is *grilled on the Hill*, legislators intensely question that person in either the House of Representatives or the Senate.

Political Parties of Legislators

Legislators belong to a specific political party. Political parties are groups formed by people with common values who unite into one political party in order to "win elections, operate government, and influence public policy."[2]

There are two major political parties in the United States: Republicans and Democrats. The Republican Party (also called the *GOP*, which stands for "Grand Old Party") is the more conservative party, and the Democratic Party is the more liberal party.

	Political Party		
	Democratic Party (Democrats)	*Republican Party (Republicans) GOP (Grand Old Party)*	
Symbol	Donkey	Elephant	
Symbolic colors	Blue — *Blue states* are those whose citizens are generally more liberal, usually favoring Democratic views.	Purple — *Purple states* have a combination of ideologies: some liberal and some conservative.	Red — *Red states* are those whose citizens are generally more conservative, usually favoring Republican views.
Political "leaning"	Liberal or Left	Conservative or Right	
Ideology, selected examples (though this varies within each party)	Prioritize • comprehensive federal regulation over states' rights • comprehensive regulation of guns over individual gun ownership • a woman's right to choose an abortion over broad governmental restrictions on abortion • individual rights of association over right to act according to religious beliefs	Prioritize • states' rights over comprehensive federal regulation • individual gun ownership over comprehensive regulation of guns • broad governmental restrictions on abortion over a woman's right to choose an abortion • the right to act according to religious beliefs over individual rights of association	

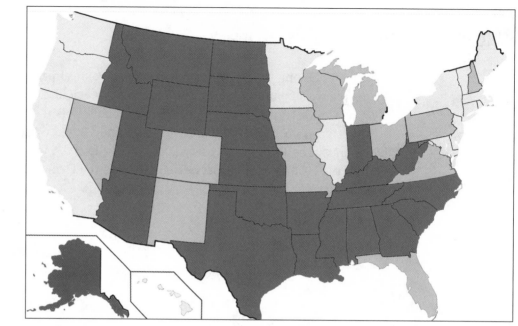

Red

Blue

Purple

Red, blue, and purple states, on the basis of the 2008 presidential election.

WORD STUDY | *Partisan, Vote along Party Lines, Political Gridlock, Majority Party, Minority Party, Polarized Congress*

Legislation can only pass in Congress when legislators gain a majority vote for a bill in both houses. The following terms may arise when discussing the ability or inability to pass new laws due to political party affiliation.

Partisan

The noun *partisan* means a person who favors one particular political party.[3] *Partisan* can also function as an adjective, as follows: a *partisan vote* means that legislators of the same political party united and voted one way (either for or against a proposed bill), and members of a different political party voted in the opposite way. Republicans may oppose certain laws limiting gun ownership, while Democrats may favor such laws. Legislators who vote according to the values of their political parties vote in a *partisan* manner.

Vote along Party Lines

Similarly, legislators who vote along with similar members of their political party *vote along party lines*, that is, in line with or in the same way as other members of the same party.

Political Gridlock

Gridlock often refers to cars that cannot move in traffic because of blocked intersections.

Political gridlock occurs when laws cannot pass because a majority of legislators from one political party vote in a partisan manner (in common with members of their political party) for a bill, and a majority of legislators from the other political party vote against a bill, blocking each other from moving forward and passing the bill.

Majority of Republicans in one house of Congress vote *Yes*	Gridlock Bill cannot pass without approval from both houses of Congress	Majority of Democrats in the other house of Congress vote *No*

Majority Party, Minority Party

* A *midterm election* is an election in the middle, or second year, of a president's four-year term. The resulting vote may shift political control to one party or the other.

Depending on the election year, either Republicans or Democrats could be the *majority party*. This means that the party holds more than one-half of the seats in the Senate (51 or more of the 100 Senate seats) or the House of Representatives (218 or more of the 435 House seats) or in both houses of Congress. The party holding less than one-half of the seats is called the *minority party*. A political party's control of the Senate and House of Representatives has a significant impact on lawmaking.*

Session of Congress	President Political party	Senate	House of Representatives
113th Congress (2013–15)	President Obama Democrat	Democratic majority 53 Democrats 45 Republicans 2 Independents	Republican majority 201 Democrats 234 Republicans
114th Congress (2015–17)	President Obama Democrat	Republican majority 44 Democrats 54 Republicans 2 Independents	Republican majority 188 Democrats 247 Republicans
115th Congress, 1st session (2017–18)	President Trump Republican	Republican majority 46 Democrats 52 Republicans 2 Independents	Republican majority 193 Democrats 238 Republicans (4 vacancies at one time)

Source: Senate.gov and House.gov

During the 114th Congress, the Republican majority in both houses of Congress sometimes disagreed with proposed legislation that President Obama, a Democrat, and the Democratic legislators supported. And even if a bill did have enough votes to pass both houses of Congress with the Republican majorities, then President Obama, a Democrat, could have decided to veto (reject) the bill.

In the 115th Congress, in 2017, there was a Republican president and a Republican majority in both houses of Congress. Despite this majority, initial efforts at repealing an important health care law failed because some Republicans supported the law. By contrast, an overhaul of the federal tax code did ultimately become law in 2017.

RESEARCH UPDATE

Consult www.Senate.gov and www.House.gov
What is the number of the current congressional session?
Is there a Republican or a Democratic majority of senators in the Senate and representatives in the House of Representatives?
Is there a Republican or Democratic president of the United States?
Has partisanship affected the ability to pass new laws?

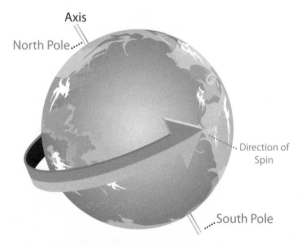

Axis
North Pole
Direction of Spin
South Pole

Polarized Congress

A Congress divided by ideological views is *polarized*. The term *polarized* relates to the adjective *polar*, which describes direct opposites. We can think of the North Pole and the South Pole, which are at opposite ends of the Earth. A *polarized* Congress is one in which senators and representatives strongly disagree on an issue, in effect positioning them at opposite ends of an issue.

EXERCISE 13 | Word Fill-In

Instructions: Fill in the blanks using the terms *partisan*, *polarization*, or *political gridlock* (one time each).

1. The bill stalled in Congress due to _____. The bill could not move through the House of Representatives or the Senate.

2. The _____ of Congress was apparent. Republican Party members were on one side, supporting the bill, and Democratic Party members were on the opposite side, not supporting the bill.

3. The bill passed in both houses of Congress after a _____ vote. Republican legislators (in the majority) supported the bill, and Democratic legislators (in the minority) opposed the bill.

WORD STUDY | *Lawmakers (Legislators) on Both Sides of the Aisle*

Democrats sit together across an aisle or pathway from Republicans, who sit together on the other side of the aisle.

This expression describes whether lawmakers either agreed or disagreed on a proposed law or another issue:

> Lawmakers on both sides of the aisle voted to confirm Sandra Day O'Connor to serve as the first woman Justice of the United States Supreme Court.

This means that there was no partisanship and that both Democrats and Republicans in the Senate, in 1981, agreed on (now retired) Justice O'Connor's qualifications to serve as an associate justice.

Congressional aisle

WORD STUDY | *Prefixes uni-, bi-, non-*

Unicycle

Uni- means "one." The following are examples of words beginning with *uni-*:

▸ *United States* refers to the country and can also mean federal.

▸ *To unify* means to bring together to act as one.

▸ *Union* means one or more people or entities joining together to become as one.

▸ As an adjective, *uniform* means one consistent way, such as *uniform rules*. The Federal Rules of Civil Procedure govern civil procedure in federal cases. These are *uniform* rules that apply consistently in federal courts throughout the entire United States. As a noun, a *uniform* is one type of clothing that people in a similar situation wear, such as police officers and students in certain schools.

Bi- means "two." The following are examples of words using the prefix *bi-*:

▸ *Bicameral* means two chambers. A *bicameral* legislature consists of two chambers or separate houses, such as the House of Representatives and the Senate that together make up Congress. Most state legislatures are *bicameral* as well, with two different chamber or houses.

▸ *Bipartisan* refers to the two major political parties in the United States. A bill that receives *bipartisan* support has received support from both the Republican and Democratic Parties.

Bicycle

Non- means "not, without, or lacking." The following are examples of words using the prefix *non-*:

▸ *Nonpartisan* means without a political affiliation or interest. A *nonpartisan* group is neutral in political ideology and works independently, without being influenced by either Democratic or Republican interests.

▸ *Nonprofit* means not for monetary gain or profit. A *nonprofit* group, such as a museum, exists to serve the public interest and not to make money (profits).

EXERCISE 14 | Prefixes uni-, bi-, non-

Instructions: Fill in the blanks with the correct prefix: *uni-, bi-, or non-*.

1. There are two chambers of Congress: the Senate and the House of Representatives. Congress is _____ cameral.

2. There is only one federal government, also called the _____ted States government.

3. The state of Nebraska has just one legislative chamber: it is _____cameral.

4. The two political parties, the Democrats and the Republicans (GOP), agreed that there should be federal drone* regulation. Drone regulation received _____ partisan support.

5. The Human Rights Watch and certain museums, such as the Museum of Modern Art, do not seek to make profits; both are famous _____profit organizations.

6. The Government Accounting Office (GAO) does not have a particular political party affiliation and is a _____ partisan group.

7. The Preamble to the Federal Constitution set forth the Founding Fathers' goals in setting up the _____ted States government. One goal was to create a strong central government in order to _____fy the states and "form a more perfect _____on" of the separate states.

8. The federal government often seeks to enforce _____form rules that apply equally throughout the United States, such as food safety, air safety, and national defense.

* A drone is an airborne device, without a pilot, that is controlled from the ground and used for surveillance and other purposes. Another name for drone is *unmanned aerial vehicle, or UAV* for short.

The Powers of the Federal Legislature

Article I, Section 8 (§ 8),* of the Federal Constitution specifically enumerates (lists) the powers of the federal legislature. Granting powers is, in effect, a limit on powers[4] because Article I, § 8, gives Congress limited powers to legislate only on specific subjects or types of laws. Thus, a party during a court case can challenge the constitutionality of a law, requesting that the court *strike down* or *invalidate* a law as unconstitutional on the ground that Congress (or another branch) exceeded its constitutionally granted powers when enacting that law.**

The following are excerpts from Congress's Article I, § 8, enumerated powers. Brackets identify each separate *clause* number, such as the Article I, § 8, clause 1, taxing clause. Square brackets ([]) are inserted before and after each number because these clause numbers do not appear in the original text. When adding text to a quotation in legal writing, brackets show an alteration from the original.

The Congress shall have Power

[1] To lay and collect Taxes, Duties, Imposts and Excises, to pay the Debts and provide for the common Defence and general Welfare of the United States;

[2] To borrow Money on the credit of the United States;

[3] To regulate Commerce with foreign Nations, and among the several States, and with the Indian Tribes;

[4] To establish an uniform Rule of Naturalization, and uniform Laws on the subject of Bankruptcies throughout the United States;

[5] To coin Money, regulate the Value thereof, and of foreign Coin . . . ;

[6] To provide for the Punishment of counterfeiting the Securities and current Coin of the United States;

[7] To establish Post Offices and post Roads;

[8] To promote the Progress of Science and useful Arts, by securing for limited Times to Authors and Inventors the exclusive Right to their respective Writings and Discoveries;

[9] To constitute Tribunals inferior to the supreme Court;

[10] To define and punish Piracies and Felonies committed on the high Seas . . . ;

[11] To declare War . . . ;

[12] To raise and support Armies . . . ;

[13] To provide and maintain a Navy;

[14] To make Rules for the Government and Regulation of the land and naval Forces;

[15] To provide for calling forth the Militia to execute the Laws of the Union, suppress Insurrections and repel Invasions;

[16] To provide for organizing, arming, and disciplining, the Militia . . . ;

[17] To exercise exclusive Legislation in all Cases whatsoever, over such District . . . ;

[18] To make all Laws which shall be necessary and proper for carrying into Execution the foregoing Powers, and all other Powers vested by this Constitution in the Government of the United States.

EXERCISE 15 | # Federal Enumerated Legislative Powers

Instructions: Match the laws in the first column with the corresponding Article I, § 8, enumerated legislative power from this and the previous page. Give a citation for the specific clause in the right-hand column, following the model in the first item.

Laws	Constitutional Authority and Citation
1. Bankruptcy laws protecting people who have no money from creditors to whom they may owe money	U.S. Const. art. I, § 8, cl. 4.
2. Copyright laws protecting creators of artistic creations such as movies, songs, books, articles, and art forms	
3. Criminal laws proscribing the transportation of a stolen car in interstate commerce, across state lines	
4. Laws prescribing the draft age when a person can serve in the army or other division of the armed forces	
5. Laws governing when a person can become a US citizen	
6. Patent laws protecting scientists and others who invent new medicines and other scientific advances	
7. Counterfeiting laws prohibiting the unlawful printing of US currency	
8. Laws governing the payment of federal taxes and prohibiting federal tax evasion	

WORD STUDY | *Prescribe, Proscribe*

Prescribe means to state or specify. *Proscribe* means to forbid or to prohibit.

In number 4 in exercise 15 on the previous page, *prescribe* refers to laws that state or specify how old a person has to be to serve in the armed forces. In number 3 in exercise 15, *proscribe* refers to a forbidden or prohibited act, here the crime prohibiting the transportation of stolen vehicles in interstate commerce.

WORD STUDY | *Enumerated, Concurrent, and Reserved Powers*

The extent of legislative powers and the balance of power between the federal, state, and local governments when enacting laws are recurring issues in the United States, with many detailed rules. In general, the principles of *reserved, enumerated, concurrent,* and *police* powers guide courts in determining which level of government has the power to enact a specific law and are summarized in the following chart.

	Power: level of government		
	Enumerated (listed) powers: federal government (may or may not be exclusive)	*Concurrent powers: federal, state, and local governments share*	*Reserved powers: states only*
Definitions	Powers that are specifically numbered or listed in Article I, Section 8, of the Federal Constitution	Powers that are shared concurrently (at the same time) by the levels of governments	Powers that are reserved or specifically left to the fifty states
Descriptions	These powers give Congress authority to enact specific types of law affecting the entire nation.	Each level of governments needs these powers to function properly.	These powers allow the states to enact laws on more local matters, the importance of which may vary from state to state.
Examples	Under the Federal Constitution, Congress has the power "to establish . . . uniform Laws on the subject of bankruptcies throughout the United States." U.S. Const. Art. I § 8, cl. 4. Bankruptcy laws are federal laws, and bankruptcy courts are part of the system of federal courts.	All federal, state, and local governments need money to pay for essential services. Thus, federal, state, and local governments all have the power to tax.	State laws define state (and not federal) crimes and typically regulate wills, estates, marriage, divorce, education, and adoption. Some state powers are sometimes called *police powers.* Reserved powers have their source in the United States Constitution.*

* "The powers not delegated to the United States by the Constitution, nor prohibited by it to the States, are reserved to the States respectively, or to the people." U.S. Const. amend. 10.

EXERCISE 16 | Powers of the Federal and State Governments in Context

Background: In 2012, the United States Supreme Court analyzed whether Congress had the constitutional power to enact a law making major changes to health care in the United States. The case involved the constitutionality of a 2010 statute that Congress enacted, called in part the Patient Protection and Affordable Care Act (PPACA), Public Law No. 111-148.

The statute is known colloquially as "Obamacare," named for President Obama, who sought to greatly expand health care to people throughout the United States. One part of the statute required that most Americans in every state purchase health insurance or pay a penalty, called the "individual mandate."[5]

The plaintiffs in the case—the National Federation of Independent Business and others—sued several government defendants, including Kathleen Sebelius, then secretary of Health and Human Services (HHS). HHS is the agency responsible for administering (carrying out) health care policy. Plaintiffs asserted that Congress did not have the constitutional power to enact this federal statute.

The United States government claimed, in part, that the commerce clause (Art. I, § 8, cl. 3) and the taxing clause (Art. I, § 8, cl. 1) gave Congress the power to enact this statute.[6] Ultimately, the court decided that the taxing clause authorized Congress to enact this statute; citizens had to state on their tax returns if they had health insurance coverage, and if they did not, they had to pay the individual mandate penalty.

Instructions: The following selected excerpts from *National Federation of Independent Business v. Sebelius*, 567 U.S. 519, 530–37 (2012), are followed by questions about each specific excerpt. Read the text and then answer the corresponding questions.

Chief Justice Roberts delivered the opinion of the Court:

Today we resolve constitutional challenges to two provisions of the Patient Protection and Affordable Care Act of 2010: the individual mandate, which requires individuals to purchase a health insurance policy providing a minimum level of coverage; and the Medicaid expansion, which gives funds to the States on the condition that they provide specified health care to all citizens whose income falls below a certain threshold. We do not consider whether the Act embodies sound policies. That judgment is entrusted to the Nation's elected leaders. We ask only whether Congress has the power under the Constitution to enact the challenged provisions.

1. How does this first paragraph illustrate the principle of separation of powers?

In our federal system, the National Government possesses only limited powers; the States and the people retain the remainder. . . . In this case we must again determine whether the Constitution grants Congress powers it now asserts, but which many States and individuals believe it does not possess. Resolving this controversy requires us to examine both the limits of the Government's power, and our own limited role in policing those boundaries.

The Federal Government "is acknowledged by all to be one of enumerated powers." *Ibid.* That is, rather than granting general authority to perform all the conceivable functions of government, the Constitution lists, or enumerates, the Federal Government's powers. Congress may, for example, "coin Money," "establish Post Offices," and "raise and support Armies." Art. I, § 8, cls. 5, 7, 12. The enumeration of powers is also a limitation of powers, because "[t]he enumeration presupposes something not enumerated." *Gibbons v. Ogden*, 9 Wheat. 1, 195 (1824). The Constitution's express conferral of some powers makes clear that it does not grant others. And the Federal Government "can exercise only the powers granted to it." *McCulloch, supra*, at 405.

2. What powers does the national (federal) government possess?

3. What is a synonym for "enumerated"?

4. What are "enumerated powers," and what examples of enumerated powers does Chief Justice Roberts give?

5. Is the federal government a government of limited powers? Why is this important?

Today, the restrictions on government power foremost in many Americans' minds are likely to be affirmative prohibitions, such as contained in the Bill of Rights.[7] These affirmative prohibitions come into play, however, only where the Government possesses authority to act in the first place. If no enumerated power authorizes Congress to pass a certain law, that law may not be enacted, even if it would not violate any of the express prohibitions in the Bill of Rights or elsewhere in the Constitution.

6. What are some examples of "affirmative prohibitions" in the Bill of Rights (see in appendix 1) If a law does not violate any of these "affirmative prohibitions," does Congress have unfettered (unlimited) ability to pass that law?

Reserved Powers
_____

Indeed, the Constitution did not initially include a Bill of Rights at least partly because the Framers felt the enumeration of powers sufficed to restrain the Government. As Alexander Hamilton put it, "the Constitution is itself, in every rational sense, and to every useful purpose, A BILL OF RIGHTS." The Federalist No. 84, p. 515 (C. Rossiter ed. 1961). And when the Bill of Rights was ratified, it made express what the enumeration of powers necessarily implied: "The powers not delegated to the United States by the Constitution . . . are reserved to the States respectively, or to the people." U.S. Const., Amdt. 10. The Federal Government has expanded dramatically over the past two centuries, but it still must show that a constitutional grant of power authorizes each of its actions. See, *e.g., United States v. Comstock*, 560 U.S. 126 (2010).

The same does not apply to the States, because the Constitution is not the source of their power. The Constitution may restrict state governments—as it does, for example, by forbidding them to deny any person the equal protection of the laws. But where such prohibitions do not apply, state governments do not need constitutional authorization to act. The States thus can and do perform many of the vital functions of modern government—punishing street crime, running public schools, and zoning property for development, to name but a few—even though the Constitution's text does not authorize any government to do so. Our cases refer to this general power of governing, possessed by the States but not by the Federal Government, as the "police power." See, *e.g.*, *United States v. Morrison*, 529 U.S. 598, 618–19 (2000).

Police Powers

─────────────────

7. **Which powers do the states have, and what is the source of this power?**

8. **How does the Constitution restrict state governments?**

State sovereignty is not just an end in itself: Rather, federalism secures to citizens the liberties that derive from the diffusion of sovereign power." *New York v. United States*, 505 U.S. 144, 181, (1992) (internal quotation marks omitted). Because the police power is controlled by 50 different States instead of one national sovereign, the facets of governing that touch on citizens' daily lives are normally administered by smaller governments closer to the governed. The Framers thus ensured that powers which "in the ordinary course of affairs, concern the lives, liberties, and properties of the people" were held by governments more local and more accountable than a distant federal bureaucracy. The Federalist No. 45, at 293 (J. Madison). The independent power of the States also serves as a check on the power of the Federal Government: "By denying any one government complete jurisdiction over all the concerns of public life, federalism protects the liberty of the individual from arbitrary power." *Bond v. United States*, 564 U.S. 211, 222 (2011).

9. **Why did the framers ensure that the states retain these powers?**

The principles of enumerated, concurrent, and reserved powers (and others) define certain powers that the different levels of government have to enact specific types of laws. But even when there is an enumerated federal power authorizing Congress to legislate, states and local governments may also be able to legislate in a particular area. When there is a conflict between federal, state, and local legislation, which laws prevail?

Preemption is a principle that federal law is supreme and controls over conflicting state and local laws. The Federal Constitution's supremacy clause states in Article VI, clause 2,

Federal

|

State/local

> This Constitution, and the Laws of the United States which shall be made in pursuance thereof; and all Treaties made, or which shall be made under the Authority of the United States, shall be the supreme Law of the Land; and the Judges in every State shall be bound thereby, any Thing in the Constitution or Laws of any State to the Contrary notwithstanding.

In contemporary US society, the conflict between federal, state, and local laws arises when states or local governments may seek greater or different protections for their own residents. There are several *hot-button issues* (and other issues) in which the conflict between the levels of government powers to regulate arises.

WORD STUDY | *Hot-Button Issue*

A *hot-button issue* is one that is important to people and evokes strong emotions. The name could symbolize pressing a button that is extremely hot and that people therefore might not want to touch.

Three current *hot-button issues* of critical importance in US society are marijuana enforcement, immigration, and gun control. Congress has the power to regulate these areas under Article I, § 8, but states legislate or act in these areas as well. It is important to research any changes to laws and their enforcement under the current administration.

* *Gonzales v. Raich*, 545 U.S. 1 (2005), upheld Congress's power to regulate *intrastate* medical marijuana production under the commerce clause.

1. Marijuana laws. Federal laws* prohibit marijuana (known colloquially as "pot") distribution, but many states have legalized marijuana for either medical or recreational purposes, or both, causing a conflict.[8] The executive branch enforces the laws, and under President Obama, the administration exercised "enforcement discretion to allow . . . state policy experiments to play out"[9] when legalizing marijuana, resulting in the lack of enforcement of these federal laws.

2. Immigration. The conflict between federal authorities seeking to enforce immigration laws and state and local governments is the source of ongoing litigation. Some states and cities have declared themselves as a "sanctuary state" or a "sanctuary city." A sanctuary is a place that provides protection from danger. In the immigration

context, a sanctuary state or city protects people who are not legally in the United States (undocumented) from federal agents who will arrest them and attempt to remove them from the United States.

3. Gun control. With exceptions, Congress has not preempted state or local gun regulation.[10] And despite the fact that laws regulating gun possession could fall to local governments, which generally have the power to regulate "public health, safety and welfare," some states have removed local authorities' power to pass gun laws[11] since states may also preempt local laws within that particular state. This area of law is also a source of current litigation.

Gun-control laws* vary, and permissible gun regulation is a source of much debate and partisan divides, especially because of the many incidents of gun violence in the United States, such as the tragic loss of lives at Sandy Hook Elementary School in Newtown, Connecticut, where twenty young children (six and seven years of age) and six adults were killed; in Orlando, Florida, where forty-nine people were killed in a nightclub; in Las Vegas, Nevada, where fifty-eight people attending an outdoor concert were killed; and in Parkland, Florida, where seventeen people were killed, including high school students and teachers. Numerous others were wounded in these incidents.

This proliferation of gun violence has caused strong protests and calls for legislatures to enact stronger gun laws in blue and some purple states and cities where many citizens favor strict gun control. By contrast, in Texas, and other red, conservative states, many people favor strong individual rights to own guns and believe that having guns protects citizens because law enforcement officers and others who have a gun can stop a person who is shooting others and thereby prevent further deaths.

* *McDonald v. Chicago*, 561 U.S. 742 (2010), held that the Second Amendment "right to bear arms" applies to the states and not just the federal government.

LESSON 2.4 The Federal Legislature's Source of Law

Congress enacts federal laws, which are more specifically called *statutes*.* Depending on the political parties and the number of Republican or Democratic lawmakers supporting or opposing a bill, political gridlock in a polarized Congress could make it difficult to enact statutes.

On the federal level, senators in the Senate or representatives in the House hear about a problem facing their constituents (the people whom they represent in their home states) and then write and introduce in either house of Congress proposed legislation designed to address this problem. Proposed legislation is called a *bill* when it is presented to the legislature and may be named for the originator, or sponsor, of the bill.

WORD STUDY | *Pass a Law, Pass Legislation, Enact a Law, Act, Legislation, Statute, Bill, Proposed Legislation, Sign into Law*

When Congress *passes a law (bill)*, or *passes legislation*, this means that the legislative body has voted favorably on (approved) the bill. The bill then moves to the federal executive. One way that a bill can then become a law, or *enacted*, is when the executive, the president, approves of and *signs the bill into law*. (A bill that passes a state legislature is then sent to the state executive, the governor, and a bill that passes a local legislature may be sent to the local executive, the mayor or other, depending on the governing local rules.) Notice the word *act* within the verb *enact*. An *act* is the official (often popular) name for an enacted law. In the *Statutes at Large*, shown later in this lesson, there are several examples of enacted laws and their popular names.

Law has a specific meaning here: the source of law from the legislature, also called *legislation* or *statute*. Legislation that has not yet become law is first called a *bill*, also known as *proposed legislation*. Legislators first present a bill to one single legislative house (the Senate or the House of Representatives on the federal level) or simultaneously in both houses.

Law outside of this context could be from any of the three branches of government, but *legislation* and *statute* refer only to the source of law from a legislature.

Here is an overview of the path of a bill through Congress, omitting several potential steps in this process for simplification purposes:

1. A legislator introduces a bill

A senator or a representative (now called the bill's *sponsor*) introduces the proposed bill in his or her own chamber of Congress.

Bills are assigned a number. The first bill of each Congress (two-year period) introduced in the Senate is numbered S. 1, and in the House, it is H.R. 1.

2. Committee and subcommittee hearings and report

The bill is referred to a relevant committee and often to a subcommittee for review and hearings. Experts and others can testify at the hearing, and legislators can subpoena* witnesses to appear.

A bill can pass or die in committee.

3. Floor debate and vote

If a bill passes the committee, it is sent to the floor of the originating house of Congress for the consideration and vote of all of the legislators present.

4. The second house considers the bill

A bill originating in the Senate would then be considered in the House of Representatives, and a bill originating in the House of Representatives would then be considered in the Senate. The second house would conduct committee and subcommittee review, and if the bill passes the committee, it would be sent to the floor for debate and vote.

5. The bill is sent to the president of the United States

If a bill passes both chambers of Congress, it is sent to the president. The bill becomes law if the president approves it by signing the bill into law or failing to sign the bill within ten days after it is presented to him (excluding Sundays, assuming Congress has not adjourned during this period).

If the president rejects the bill (called a *veto*), it is sent back to the originating house, which can override the veto by a two-thirds vote of both chambers of Congress. U.S. Const. art. I, § 7.

---

* A *subpoena* is a document issued in certain proceedings that requires the recipient to produce documents, give testimony, or both. Refusal to comply with a subpoena can result in *contempt* proceedings.

Legislative History

Legislators can introduce a bill in either chamber, or house, of Congress or in both chambers simultaneously. But every bill must move through, and then pass, or be approved by, both houses of Congress before the president receives the bill.

When the bill is moving through Congress, different committees and subcommittees vet (scrutinize or closely examine) it. (See Step 2 in the table on the previous page.) Committees are groups of legislators who hold hearings on subject matter that falls within that committee's jurisdiction (power). For instance, the United States Senate Committee on the Judiciary holds hearings on the qualifications of Supreme Court justices and ambassadors whom the president nominates.[12] The United States Senate Committee on Commerce, Science, and Transportation has jurisdiction over bills regulating US highways, interstate commerce, and scientific research and development.[13]

Specific documents reflect the bill's history as it moves through Congress, during the process described in Steps 2 and 3 of the table, including why the law was proposed and what areas the bill covers. Examples of these documents are

1. committee *reports*, which typically explain the need for and purpose of a bill;
2. transcripts of committee hearings of witness testimony; and
3. transcripts of floor debates, which record legislators' support for or opposition to a bill.

Collectively, these written documents record the *legislative history* for a statute.

Judges may look to legislative history when interpreting the terms of a statute during a single court case because Congress, and not the courts, has the constitutional power to enact statutes. In doing so, judges are, in effect, seeking guidance from the branch of government that is constitutionally charged with legislating, as to what the intended purpose of that statute is and how to interpret a statutory term. If the *plain meaning*[14] of a statutory term is not clear from the specific words Congress uses in the statute, a judge may look to the statute's legislative history for further guidance. A judge might ask, "What was the legislature's intent when enacting this statute?" Interestingly, some judges and scholars believe that legislative history, which is susceptible to different interpretations, should not necessarily guide the interpretation of statutes.[15]

The legislative history document that follows records the House's reasons for passing a federal criminal law. In later court cases, when a defendant is charged with violating this law, a court could review this document to determine the meaning of the statutory term *motor vehicle* and what Congress intended to proscribe when passing the law.

66th Congress, 1st Session.	} HOUSE OF REPRESENTATIVES. {	REPORT No. 312.

THEFT OF AUTOMOBILES

SEPTEMBER 12, 1919.—Referred to the House Calendar and ordered to be printed

Mr. DYER, from the Committee on the Judiciary, submitted the following

REPORT.

[To Accompany H.R. 9203.]

The Committee on the Judiciary, to whom was referred the bill (H.R. 9203) to punish the transportation of stolen motor vehicles in interstate or foreign commerce, having considered the same, report thereon with a recommendation that it pass.

The Congress of the United States can scarcely enact any law at this session that is more needed than the bill herein recommended, and that has for its purpose the providing of severe punishment of those guilty of the stealing of automobiles in interstate or foreign commerce. There has been and is now a most widespread demand for such a law. State laws upon the subject have been inadequate to meet the evil. Thieves steal automobiles and take them from one State to another and ofttimes have associates in this crime who receive and sell the stolen machines. The losses to the people of the United States by reason of this stealing amounts to hundreds of thousands of dollars every year. It is getting worse. It is getting so now that it is difficult for the owners of the cheaper cars to obtain theft insurance, due to the great loss that insurance companies have sustained. During the past year automobile-theft insurance on this class of cars has increased 100 per cent. It is automobiles of that price that are generally stolen. Automobile thieves who make a specialty of this crime do not steal many of the higher priced cars, the reason being of course that they are not so easily sold. I submit the following table in proof of the above statement relative to the increased cost, etc., of automobile-theft insurance:

Comparative statement showing increase in cost of automobile theft insurance between June 1, 1918, and June 1, 1919.

	Class A, $3,500 and up		Class B, $2,500–$3,499		Class C, $1,800–$2499		Class D, $799–$1,799		Class E, $799 and under.	
	1918	1919	1918	1919	1918	1919	1918	1919	1918	1919
New Cars ...	$0.50	$0.25	$0.75	$0.60	$1.00	$1.00	$1.75	$3.00	$2.75	$5.00
1 year old ...	.50	.25	.75	.60	1.00	.90	1.50	2.75	2.25	4.00
2 years old ...	.50	.25	.75	.60	.75	.75	1.25	2.40	1.25	3.00
3 years old ...	.50	.25	.75	.60	.75	.60	1.00	1.90	1.25	2.50

NOTE.—It will be noticed that the increase in cost of theft insurance on cars selling at $799 (f. o. b.) and under has increased approximately 100 per cent in the period between June, 1918, and June, 1919, while cars on class D, $799 to $1,799, shows a correspondingly large increase.

Thieves have found the automobile field one in which they can reap huge harvests, due to the fact no doubt that there are so many automobiles and trucks registered in the United States. On July 1, 1919, the number of automobiles and trucks registered to the United States amounted to a total of 6,353,233. July and August are always heavy selling months. It is therefore quite certain that the number of automobiles now in use has increased to approximately 6,500,000 cars, with an average estimated value of $1,200 each, giving a total value for all cars now in use at $7,800,000,000. I submit the following table showing how these cars are distributed according to States, as of July 1 last.

Cars and trucks in United States, July 1, 1919.
[All duplicate registrations deducted.]

Ohio	464,826
New York	436,932
Pennsylvania	407,923
Illinois	401,371
California	349,734
Iowa	276,500
Michigan	273,396
Texas	249,346
Indiana	246,000
Minnesota	229,570
Wisconsin	212,490
Massachusetts	210,063
Kansas	206,033
Missouri	201,484
Nebraska	183,000
New Jersey	144,763
Washington	125,219
Oklahoma	124,501
Georgia	115,454
South Dakota	91,808
Colorado	88,315
Connecticut	85,200
Tennessee	84,000
Virginia	82,000
North Carolina	79,475
Maryland	75,590
Kentucky	75,259
North Dakota	73,015
Oregon	65,417
South Carolina	59,000
Alabama	55,402
Montana	53,420
Florida	48,598
Louisiana	46,150
West Virginia	45,019
Maine	43,656
Arkansas	43,238
Mississippi	39,399
District of Columbia	37,928
Idaho	35,817
Utah	30,760
New Hampshire	26,230
Rhode Island	26,112
Arizona	24,298
Vermont	22,094
Wyoming	18,200
New Mexico	16,875
Delaware	14,200
Nevada	8,153
Total	6,353,233

The total number of cars reported stolen in 18 western and mid-western cities during 1918 was 22,273. The city of Detroit, Mich., headed the list with 2,637 cars stolen; Chicago came second with 2,611, and St. Louis third, with 2,241. Kansas City, Mo., led in the list with a total percentage of cars not recovered, 46 per cent. St. Louis was second with forty per cent of cars being lost absolutely. The following table gives, in addition to the cities mentioned, the record of the other 18 cities referred to:

Record of stolen cars in 18 cities.

	Stolen.	Recovered.
Chicago	2,611	1,954
St. Louis	2,211	1,354
Kansas City	1,144	606
Denver	901	627
Omaha	1.039	669
Columbus, Ohio	451	352
Cincinnati	348	291
San Francisco	1,122	1,082
Los Angeles	1,629	1,499
Oakland	805	860
Seattle	1,451	1,376
Portland	1,088	990
Salt Lake City	797	790
Boston	856	607
Detroit	2,607	1,834
Indianapolis	404	....
Oklahoma City	571	484
Cleveland	2,076	1,816

The power of the Congress to enact this law and to punish the theft of automobiles in one State and the removing of them into another State can not be questioned, in view of laws of similar nature heretofore enacted by Congress and the decisions of the Supreme Court of the United States touching same.

The purpose of the commerce clause in the Constitution was to regulate and promote the freedom of commercial intercourse between the States and foreign nations. The power granted under this clause is absolute and practically without qualification. Commerce has frequently been defined by the court as "intercourse," but not all intercourse is commerce. To render intercourse commerce there must be present the element of transportation. Transportation is essential to commerce or rather is commerce itself, and the commodities transported may be tangible or intangible. Neither are they limited to those known at the time of adoption of the Constitution.

Legislative history: a report of the House of Representatives submitted by Representative Dyer of the House Committee on the Judiciary, in H.R. Rep. No. 66-312 (1919). "66" in the report number, "66-312," refers to the 66th Congress, a congressional session, as lesson 2.2 describes. Read the report excerpts to learn why Congress proposed this federal law. Page 3 of the report (*bottom left*) discusses the "power of Congress to enact this law." Which enumerated power does the report refer to?

WORD STUDY | *Statute, Statue, United States Code (U.S.C.)*

A *statute* is the source of law from a legislature.

Congress enacts federal statutes, which are printed in the *United States Code* (U.S.C.). Notice the U.S.C. abbreviations after descriptions of the following statutes. Recall that *United States* (*US*) can be a synonym for *federal*. The terms *United States* in *United States Code* inform us that this is a federal (as opposed to a state or local) statute.

Here are sample federal statutes:

▸ The National Motor Vehicle Theft Act, from 1919, prohibited a person from transporting in interstate or foreign commerce a motor vehicle, knowing the vehicle to have been stolen. 18 U.S.C. § 408(3).

▸ The Gun Free School Zone Act proscribes the possession of certain guns within 1,000 feet of a school zone. 18 U.S.C. § 922(q)(2)(A).

▸ The 2010 Patient Protection and Affordable Care Act expanded US health care. 42 U.S.C. § 18001, et seq.*

▸ The Federal Intelligence Surveillance Act (FISA) regulates electronic surveillance and searches by the federal government in the interests of national security. 50 U.S.C. §§ 1801–11.**

---

* *et seq.* means "and following," here meaning § 18002 and other sections of law following § 18001.

** As shown here, to cite or refer to more than one section of a particular statute, use two section marks: §§ 1801–11.

A *statue* is a specific type of art.

Senators and representatives from each of the fifty states represent constituents in Congress. A beautiful illustration of how each state has a separate identity, but when the states are put together, they represent the nation as a whole, is located in the Capitol Visitors Center in Congress, on Capitol Hill, in Washington, DC. In a long hallway, each state has a statue of a famous historic figure or resident representing that state, one next to the other. Here are two sample state statues located in Congress:

Alabama's statue is of Helen Keller, who was deaf and blind and became an inspirational advocate for others. She revolutionized education and communication for deaf and blind persons.

Hawaii's statue is of King Kamehameha I, a former ruler of the Hawaiian Islands.

WORD STUDY | *Vest, Vet, Scrutinize, Vent*

Vest, as a verb, means to give power or authority to act. Articles I, II, and III of the US Constitution vest different powers in three different branches of the federal government, giving Congress the power to legislate, the executive branch the power to execute the laws, and the federal judiciary (United States Supreme Court and other lower federal courts that Congress creates) the power to adjudicate.

In the following descriptions, the noun and the adjective forms are *legislature* (noun) and *legislative* (adjective), *executive* (both noun and adjective), and *judiciary* (noun) and *judicial* (adjective). The adjectives modify the noun *powers*.

The Federal Constitution *vests*

1. *legislative* powers in the *legislature*;
2. *executive* powers in the *executive*; and
3. *judicial* powers in the *judiciary*.

The verbs *vet* and *scrutinize* mean to closely examine. For instance, after a legislator proposes a bill, a congressional committee holds hearings to vet or to scrutinize the bill, that is, to examine the purpose for and wording of a law and discuss whether Congress has the Article I, § 8, power to enact that law. As one example, the House Committee on the Judiciary vetted (carefully examined) the National Motor Vehicle Theft Act, as illustrated in the House report shown earlier.

The Senate (and not the House of Representatives) has the constitutional power to vet the qualifications of an ambassador, a public minister, or a United States Supreme Court justice[16] to determine if that person is competent to serve in office. The Senate Committee on the Judiciary holds a hearing in which the senators question the nominee about his or her education, work experience, and views on important issues. Committee members may call others to testify about the nominee's qualifications as well.

The term *vet* may also be used in classes. Students may hear a professor state that the class will *vet an issue*, which means that the issue will be closely examined: there will be a detailed discussion analyzing that issue.

To *vent* means to release, as in releasing anger or frustration. Constituents protest and vent anger in order to persuade legislators to change what the constituents view as unfair or harmful laws or government actions.

EXERCISE 17 | Words in Context

Instructions: Fill in the blanks with the correct term: *vest, vet,* or *vent*. You may change the word form to make the sentence grammatical and use a word more than once.

1. The company's Board of Directors decided to _____ power in a new chief operating officer.

2. The United States Supreme Court had to _____ the issue of whether Congress had the power to enact a uniform national health care law.

3. The Fed will _____ the pros and cons of raising interest rates.

4. Some people post to Twitter to _____ their anger over different issues.

5. Congress _____ the power to investigate workplace safety in the Occupational Safety and Health Administration (OSHA), a federal administrative agency.

6. The Contracts professor decided to _____ the issue of whether the email between the parties created a valid contract.

7. Several states challenged President Trump's executive order, directing immigration officials to _____ people from certain countries who enter the United States in order to ensure that they do not pose national security risks.

8. Protestors gathered throughout the United States in order to _____ their frustration over Congress's and state legislatures' failure to enact stricter gun laws protecting people from military-style assault weapons. Others disagreed, asserting that the Second Amendment to the United States Constitution _____ strong powers in the people "to keep and bear arms." U.S. Const. amend. II.

EXERCISE 18 | Words in Context

Instructions: Read the words in context, and then answer the following questions.

Congress **vetted** a federal statute governing the possession of firearms near schools, called the Gun Free School Zones Act, by holding hearings and then making findings and declarations in order to clarify the purpose and justification for the law, as exemplified here:

> [F]irearms and ammunition move easily in interstate commerce and have been found in increasing numbers in and around schools, as documented in numerous hearings in

both the Committee on the Judiciary, the House of Representatives and the Committee on the Judiciary of the Senate. 18 U.S.C. § 922(q)(1)(C).

These committees, in the two separate houses of Congress, held hearings to determine a legislative solution to a national gun problem.

1. Which enumerated power purportedly authorized Congress to enact this statute?

2. Which congressional committees in which houses of Congress vetted the statute?

3. Which legislative history documents may have been created during this vetting process?

WORD STUDY | ## United States Code (U.S.C.), Codify, Titles of Law, Sections of Law

42 U.S.C.

* See the complete list of titles on the House of Representatives website: http://uscode.house.gov.

United States Code: Once a federal law passes (is approved by both houses of Congress) and is signed by the president or the president did not veto or timely sign the law, it becomes part of the United States Code (U.S.C.), which contains federal statutes. Each state has its own separate set of laws; the term *U.S.C.* signifies that the statute is a federal and not a state or local statute.

To *codify* means to make part of a code. The United States Code is a set of books that contains the entire official set of federal laws. The U.S.C. organizes federal statutes by subject into *titles* of law: the title is actually a specific number, which informs the reader of the subject of that law. For example, Title 35 of the United States Code contains patent laws; a reader who sees "35 U.S.C." will know that this is the title containing federal laws regulating patents. As another example, Title 42 codifies laws relating to public health and welfare.

Selected Titles of Federal Law*

Title 1 General Provisions
Title 3 The President
Title 9 Arbitration
Title 11 Bankruptcy
Title 15 Commerce and Trade
Title 17 Copyrights
Title 18 Crimes and Criminal Procedure
Title 23 Highways
Title 26 Internal Revenue Code [tax laws]
Title 28 Judiciary and Judicial Procedure [rules governing procedures in federal courts]

Title 31 Money and Finance
Title 35 Patents
Title 38 Veterans' Benefits
Title 39 Postal Service
Title 42 The Public Health and Welfare
Title 49 Transportation

EXERCISE 19 | ## Codification of Federal Statutes

Instructions: Write the title of law that *codifies* federal statutes on the following subjects.

1. Patents, protecting certain scientific discoveries:

2. Arbitration:

3. Taxes:

4. Copyrights, protecting certain artistic creations including books, music, art, and film:

5. The president:

6. Bankruptcy:

7. Health care:

8. Federal crimes:

9. The Federal Rules of Civil Procedure, governing judicial proceedings in federal civil cases:

Citations: Sections of Law

A statutory citation is an abbreviation that informs a reader of certain information such as whether the statute is from a federal, state, or local legislature and which book the statute is printed in. The citation allows a reader to look up (locate) and read the statute.

The following citation allows a reader to find this statute in the United States Code books or online.

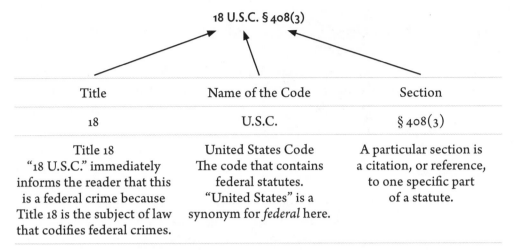

Title	Name of the Code	Section
18	U.S.C.	§ 408(3)
Title 18 "18 U.S.C." immediately informs the reader that this is a federal crime because Title 18 is the subject of law that codifies federal crimes.	United States Code The code that contains federal statutes. "United States" is a synonym for *federal* here.	A particular section is a citation, or reference, to one specific part of a statute.

Example of a statutory citation. Recall that § is a symbol for section.

EXERCISE 20 | The Legislative Process

Instructions: Start at the top of the chart and continue down to identify terminology related to the legislative process. Read the descriptions in column 1, choose one of the following nouns, and write the correct term in column 2: *bill, statute, act,*[17] *law, United States Code, title, section.* The first entry is completed as a model.

Column 1	Column 2
1. The initial form of legislation, once it is introduced in one of the houses of Congress	bill
2. The general term used to describe a bill that has passed both houses of Congress and has been signed (or not vetoed) by the president of the United States	
3. The specific term that means only a law from Congress or another legislature—a synonym is *legislation*	
4. The name for a set of laws when referred to by a popular name	
5. The name of the codified federal laws, organized by subject and printed in books and online	
6. The specific subject area for similar types of laws, such as Patents, Copyrights, or Federal Crimes	
7. The specific part of a statute, referred to by this symbol: §	

EXERCISE 21 | # Words in Context

Instructions: Read the words in context describing one statute, and then in the following sentences, which describe a different statute, fill in the blanks with the correct words from the word box. You may change the word form to make the sentence grammatical and use a word more than once.

A legislator introduced a *bill* (proposed legislation) to prohibit the possession of a firearm in a school zone. The bill *passed* both houses of Congress after receiving sufficient *bipartisan* support (a majority of legislators from both the Republican and Democratic Parties in both houses voting in favor of the bill). The bill was then sent to the president of the United States for a signature. Once the president signed the bill, it became a law and was then, more specifically, called a *statute*. Congress *enacted* the law, which is called the Gun Free School Zones *Act* of 1990.

The law was *codified*, becoming part of the United States Code (U.S.C), specifically, in Title 18, which lists federal crimes. One section of the *statute* is referred to (cited) as 18 U.S.C. § 922(q)(1)(a) and is an original version of this statute.

Word Box			
federal	legislation	act	bipartisan
bill	codifies or codified	title	passed the law

In the early 1900s, the legislator Leonidas Dyer, a representative from the state of Missouri, introduced a _____ in the House of Representatives to address an ever-increasing problem: car thieves were stealing motor vehicles and transporting them from one state to another in order to avoid prosecution in the state in which they stole the car. The bill received _____ support and was approved in both the House of Representatives and then the Senate. Congress _____, known by its popular name, the National Motor Vehicle Theft _____ and the Dyer _____ (named for Representative Dyer, the bill's sponsor). This act, when _____, became part of _____18 of the United States Code. _____ 18 of the United States Code _____ _____ crimes.

Publication of Federal Laws

In the federal system, a bill may become a law during a specific period of time or congressional session. Once a bill becomes law, it is printed in chronological (date) order in sets of books called *Statutes at Large*.

---

324   SIXTY-SIXTH CONGRESS.   SESS I.   CHS.   87-89.   1919.

October 28, 1919.
[H.R. 8980]

[Public, No.68.]

Red River.
Paris-Hugo Bridge Company
May bridge, Arthur City,
Tex.

Construction.
Vol.34, p. 84.

Amendment.

CHAP. 87. – An Act Granting the consent of Congress to the Paris-Hugo Bridge Company to contract a bridge and approaches thereto across Red River, near Arthur City, Lamar County, Texas.

Be it enacted by the Senate and House of Representatives of the United States of America in Congress assembled, That the consent of Congress is hereby granted to the Paris-Hugo Bridge Company, a corporation, and its successors and assigns to construct, maintain, and operate at a point suitable to navigation interests a bridge and approaches thereto across Red River from a point on its south bank, north of and near Arthur City, in Lamar County, Texas, to a point immediately north of said beginning and located in Choctaw County, Oklahoma, in accordance with the provisions of the Act entitles "An Act to regulate the construction of bridges over navigable waters," approved March 23, 2006.

October 29, 1919.
[H.R. 1429]

[Public, No.69.]

Public lands.
Additions to national forests
in Idaho.

Idaho National Forest.

Payette National Forest.

CHAP. 88. – An Act Adding certain lands to the Idaho National Forest and the Payette National Forest, in the State of Idaho.

Be it enacted by the Senate and House of Representatives of the United States of America in Congress assembled, That, subject to the approval of the Secretary of the Interior, all public lands in central Idaho within the tract commonly known as the Thunder Mountain region, bounded by the Idaho, Salmon, Challis, and Payette National Forests, are hereby reserved and set apart as national forest lands, as follows, subject to all laws affecting the national forests: That part of the said tract lying north of the fourth standard parallel north, Boise meridian and base, is hereby added to and made a part of the Idaho National Forest; and that part of said tract lying south of the said fourth standard parallel is hereby added to and made a part of the Payette National Forest.

Received by the President, October 17, 1919.

October 29, 1919.
[H.R. 9203]

[Public, No. 70.]
National Motor
Vehicle
Theft Act.

Definition.
"Motor vehicles."

CHAP. 89. – An Act To punish the transportation of stolen motor vehicles in interstate or foreign commerce.

Be it enacted by the Senate and House of Representatives of the United States of America in Congress assembled, That this Act may be cited as the National Motor Vehicle Theft Act.

SEC. 2. That when used in this Act:
(a) The term "motor vehicle" shall include an automobile, automobile truck, automobile wagon, motor cycle, or any other self-propelled vehicle not designed for running on rails;

SIXTY-SIXTH CONGRESS.   SESS I.   CHS.   87-89.   1919.   325

(b) The Term "interstate or foreign commerce" as used in this Act shall include transportation from one State, Territory, or the District of Columbia, to another State, Territory, or the District of Columbia, or to a foreign country, or from a foreign country to any State, Territory or the District of Columbia.

"Interstate or foreign commerce."

SEC 3. That whoever shall transport or cause to be transported in interstate or foreign commerce a motor vehicle, knowing the same to have been stolen, shall be punished by a fine of not more than $5,000, or by imprisonment of not more than five years, or both.

Punishment for transporting stolen motor vehicles

SEC. 4. That whosoever shall receive, conceal, store, barter, sell, or dispose of any motor vehicle, moving as, or which is a part of, or which constitutes interstate or foreign commerce, knowing the same to have been stolen, shall be punished by a fine of not more than $5,000, or by imprisonment of not more than five years or both.

Punishment for knowingly receiving, disposing, etc., stolen vehicle

SEC. 5. That any person violating this Act may be punished in any district in or through which such motor vehicle has been transported or removed by such offender.

Venue of prosecutions.

Received by President, October 17, 1919.

[NOTE BY THE DEPARTMENT OF STATE. – The foregoing act having been presented to the President of the United States for his approval, and not having been returned by him to the house of Congress in which it originated within the time prescribed by the Constitution of the Unites States, has become a law without his approval]

CHAP. 90. – Joint Resolution Authorizing and directing the Secretary of Agriculture to prepare and issue supplementary report on the condition of the cotton crop.

Resolved by the Senate and House of Representatives of the United States of America in Congress assembled, That the Secretary of Agriculture is hereby authorized and directed to prepare and publish not later than November 2, 1919, a supplementary estimate of the condition of the cotton crop as of the date October 25, 1919.

Received by the President, October 18, 1919.

[NOTE BY THE DEPARTMENT OF STATE. – The foregoing joint resolution having been presented to the President of the United States for his approval, and not having been returned by him to the house of Congress in which it originated within the time prescribed by the Constitution of the Unites States, has become a law without his approval]

October 30, 1919.
[H.J. Res. 230]

[Pub. Res., No.18.]

Cotton crop.
Supplementary
report directed on
condition of,
October 25, 1919

Congress passed these laws during the first session of the 66th Congress in 1919. Chapter 89 is the National Motor Vehicle Theft Act, as printed in the *Statutes at Large*. Congress vetted the act, before enactment, in the report seen on page 53. After the words "CHAP. 89—" Congress states the purpose of the act.

After publication in the *Statutes at Large,* federal laws are codified and printed in several sources, as summarized in this chart:

Name	1. United States Code (Official version)	2. United States Code Annotated (Private publisher)	3. United States Code Service (Private Publisher)
Citation	U.S.C.	U.S.C.A.	U.S.C.S.
Publisher	Government Printing Office, US House of Representatives, Office of the Law Revision Counsel	Thomson Reuters Corporation	LexisNexis (Michie)
Book and online location	Book: U.S.C. found online on the US Government Printing Office website, www.govinfo.gov[18]	Book: U.S.C.A. and online on Westlaw	Book: U.S.C.S. and online on Lexis

The United States Code (U.S.C.) is the "official version" of federal statutes because it is published under authority of the US government. The U.S.C. contains only the actual text of the federal statutes with information about the history of the statute, such as the year it was enacted and the years of any amendments. The U.S.C.A. and U.S.C.S. are "unofficial" versions of the statute, published by private publishers. They contain the text of the federal statutes, the history, and also additional references by these publishers that are useful when conducting research. For example, the U.S.C.A. and the U.S.C.S. contain references to legal resource books including legal encyclopedias, which explain the relevant section of the law and provide summaries of court decisions that have interpreted that section of law.

WORD STUDY | *Elements of a Statute*

Some statutes contain specific requirements that a party must prove in order to win a case, called the *elements* of the statute.[19]

The elements of one federal crime seen in the *Statutes at Large,* originally codified in 18 U.S.C. § 408(3)* (the National Motor Vehicle Theft Act), are listed below. The numbers 1, 2, and 3 list the three elements of the statute. In order to prove that a defendant is guilty of violating 18 U.S.C. § 408(3), the government (prosecution) must produce witness testimony or other evidence to prove all three elements of this crime.

*18 U.S.C. § 408(3) may be spoken "18 USC section four o eight three."

18 U.S.C. § 408(3)
Title 18, containing federal crimes, section 408(3), was one specific part of a statute, as follows:

1. "Whoever shall transport or cause to be transported in interstate or foreign commerce

2. a stolen motor vehicle

3. knowing the same to have been stolen

shall be punished by a fine of not more than $5,000, or by imprisonment of not more than five years, or both."

EXERCISE 22	# Elements of a Statute

* Courts may specify how a party satisfies a statute's requirements

Instructions: One federal statute, 18 U.S.C. § 922(q)(2)(A), states, "It shall be unlawful for any individual knowingly to possess a firearm that has moved in or that otherwise affects interstate or foreign commerce at a place that the individual knows, or has reasonable cause to believe, is a school zone." Deconstruct the *elements of* this section of law and write them in the boxes:*

Element #1	Element #2	Element #3
A person knowingly possessed a firearm		

WORD STUDY	*Prescribe and Proscribe Review*

Recall the differences between the verbs *prescribe* and *proscribe*.

▶ 18 U.S.C. § 922(q)(2)(A) *prescribes* (states) the penalties for possessing certain firearms in a school zone.
▶ 18 U.S.C. § 922(q)(2)(A) *proscribes* (forbids or prohibits) the possession of certain firearms in a school zone.

It is incorrect to state that a statute "proscribes penalties" because that would mean that the statute prohibits penalties.

WORD STUDY | *Prefixes inter- and intra-*

Prefixes may change the meaning of a word in a predictable way. For example, adding the prefix *inter-* predictably changes the word *state* to mean "between states" and adding the prefix *intra-* changes the word *state* to mean "within one state," because *inter-* means "between" and *intra-* means "within." Federal crimes may involve *inter-state* acts, such as transporting a motor vehicle in interstate commerce, from one state to another. State crimes may involve *intrastate acts*, such as possessing a stolen car within just one single state.

Interstate and intrastate routes in the United States.

EXERCISE 23 | ## Interstate and Intrastate

Instructions: Read the sentences and consider how the addition of the prefixes *inter-* and *intra-* change the meaning of the word *state*. Then answer the following questions.

1. A defendant is charged with transporting stolen property in *inter*state commerce. A gun has been transported in *inter*state commerce.

   Where has the property or the gun been taken? Are these federal or state crimes?

2. A defendant is charged with *intra*state transportation of stolen property.

   Where has that person taken the property? Is this a federal or state crime?

WORD STUDY | *Prefixes il-, un-, in-*

Il-, un- and –in, as prefixes, mean *not*. The following terms predictably change meaning when adding these prefixes:

- *Legal* to *illegal*, which becomes "not legal"
- *Constitutional* to *unconstitutional*, which becomes "not constitutional"
- *Tractable* to *intractable*, which means "not easy to deal with," "difficult to decide"; courts facing difficult issues may describe these as *intractable* issues

However, here are some important legal English terms with prefixes that change the meaning of the word in an unpredictable way.

Ambiguous and Unambiguous

When a term or phrase, such as one in a statute or a contract, is unclear or capable of more than one meaning, it is *ambiguous*, and when it is clear or not capable of more than one meaning, it is *unambiguous*. At first glance, it could appear that *unambiguous* means "not clear," because of the prefix *un-* meaning "not." But *unambiguous* means the opposite; it means "clear" or "capable of only one meaning."

Read the words in context:

The statute is **ambiguous**. The court must decide if an airplane is a "motor vehicle" within the meaning of the statute.

The enumeration of legislative powers is **unambiguous**. There must be an Article I, § 8, enumerated power in order for Congress to legislate.

Famous and Infamous

Someone or something that is *infamous* is actually extremely famous, often in a negative way. For example, one could describe a person who is famous for being a criminal and committing bad acts as an "infamous criminal."

Read the words in context:

Some people might say that the New York City subway system is **infamous** because it is extremely well known for its negative attributes such as dirty stations and crowded subway cars. (Others applaud this fast and convenient mode of transportation!)

Charles Manson was an **infamous** criminal. He is famous (well-known), in a negative way, for being involved with many murders.

Valuable and Invaluable

Something that is *invaluable* has a value that cannot be measured, and it is actually priceless. For example, if a person receives outstanding advice from a lawyer, one could state that the lawyer's advice was *invaluable*. This means that the advice was so valuable that it could not be measured.

Read the words in context:

The doctor gave the patient *invaluable* advice on how to stay healthy.

Other Terms Relating to Statutes: Loophole in a Statute; Close a Loophole

A loophole allows someone to slip through an opening.

A *loophole* refers to an omission or gap in a statute that allows a person or entity to avoid the statute's effect. *Closing a loophole* means to amend a statute to eliminate that gap.

In 2018, there were loopholes in gun laws that Congress had not closed. Businesses licensed under federal law to sell guns were required to conduct background checks to determine if a person may purchase a gun; but private persons who sold guns in certain states to another person online or at a gun show were not required to conduct background checks. This loophole allows certain people to buy guns without being vetted for their qualifications to own a gun. Constituents were calling on Congress to close the loophole by enacting stricter laws requiring more extensive background checks on all gun sales.

Congress did close a loophole in a different context. A federal statute, 18 U.S.C. § 1512(b)(2) prohibited a person from "inducing another person to destroy" certain documents and records. The statute did not prohibit a person from destroying documents themself. *Yates v. United States*, 574 U.S. ____, ____, 135 S. Ct. 1074, 1093 (2015) (Kagan, J., dissenting), quoting 18 U.S.C. § 1512(b)(2). Congress *closed the loophole* (gap) in the statute by enacting a new statute, 18 U.S.C. § 1519, which prohibits people from destroying certain records themselves. *Id.*

Repeal, Amend

Repeal means that a legislature revokes or cancels an entire law that is therefore no longer valid and enforceable.

Amend means that a legislature changes or alters the terms of a current law from its original form, but the law is still valid and enforceable in its amended form.[20]

Partisanship can prevent a bill from passing Congress and becoming a law. However, even after a bill becomes a law, a later Congress can seek to *amend* or *repeal* a statute. Recall that in 2010, President Obama signed the new health care law called the Affordable Care Act[21] into law. Even though, at that time, the Senate had a Democratic majority and the House of Representatives had a Republican majority, there were enough votes to pass the law in both houses of Congress.

Thereafter, President Trump (a Republican) and the GOP (Republicans) unsuccessfully sought a congressional vote to repeal (in effect, rescind or cancel) Obamacare. However, the repeal vote failed: some Republican legislators voted against the repeal bill because they represent constituents who supported Obamacare. Americans whom these lawmakers represent feared losing valued health care they had not had before and might not vote to reelect a legislator who voted to repeal this law.

When a statute is repealed, it is no longer a valid law. When a statute is amended, it is still in effect, but a legislature has changed or altered the statutory language.

RESEARCH UPDATE

Has Congress repealed Obamacare, or is the act still valid?
If Congress has not repealed Obamacare, has Congress amended it, changing the terms of the statute?

EXERCISE 24 | # Federal, State, or Local: Who Legislates?

Instructions: Federal, state, and local legislatures all have specific powers to enact laws regulating behavior. Review your answers to exercise 2 in unit 1 on governments' powers to create law. After reading this unit on the legislature, did your answers change? Review the answers to this exercise at the end of the book and look up* some of the cited laws.

* Appendix 2 describes the expression "look up" in this context.

Unit 2 Review

Instructions: Fill in the blanks with the correct words from the word box, making any necessary grammatical changes. You may use a term more than once. Then fill in the elements of the quoted statute.

Word Box			
concurrent powers	enumerated powers	commerce clause	Congress
Capitol Hill (The Hill)	partisanship	bill	capital
vet	federal	political gridlock	codify
U.S.C.	U.S.C.A.	title	section
pass laws	polarized	elements	U.S.C.S.
reserved powers	law	statute	legislate

The two houses of the federal legislature, together, are called _____, which is located on _____ in the US _____, Washington, DC. The federal legislature has limited powers and can only act in accordance with the _____ granted to it in the Constitution. One example of these limited powers is the _____. Powers that only states have are called _____, and those powers shared by the several levels of government are called _____. _____ is a noun meaning "favoring one political party," and this may cause _____ in a _____ Congress. This inability to _____ prevents Congress from fulfilling its constitutional duty to _____. If a _____ received bipartisan support, this means that both political parties favored this measure. Congress _____ proposed legislation by holding hearings in congressional committees. If a bill passes both houses of Congress and is signed by the president, it becomes a _____, which has a specific meaning here of _____. Federal statutes are _____ and printed in the official version of the statutes, called the _____.

The unofficial federal code versions are the _____ and the
_____.

_____ are specific requirements that a party must prove in a case, as
in the following _____ statute:

> Whoever knowingly aims the beam of a laser pointer at an aircraft . . . or at the flight
> path of such an aircraft, shall be fined under this title or imprisoned not more than 5
> years, or both. 18 U.S.C. § 39A(a).

The number 18 in the citation is the _____ number of federal law, and
the § symbol refers to the specific _____ of law.

Fill in the elements of the statute:

1.	2.	Potential Punishment: Fine or prison for not more than five years. (The potential punishment is not an element of the statute that the prosecution must prove. Legislatures define the criminal penalties, such as the potential length of imprisonment, and include those in statutes.)

UNIT 3   The Federal Executive

LESSON 3.1 The Constitutional Authority for the Federal Executive

Article II, § 1, of the United States Constitution vests federal executive powers as follows:

> The executive Power shall be vested in a President of the United States of America. He shall hold his Office during the Term of four Years . . . together with the Vice President, chosen for the same Term.

The White House in Washington, DC. The executive branch executes (carries out or enforces) the laws.

The president of the United States is the head of the executive branch and lives at the White House near Constitution Avenue in the nation's capital, Washington, DC.

EXERCISE 25 | Word Forms

Instructions: Define each of the following terms and write the word's part of speech, either noun, adjective, or verb. Then fill in the blanks in the sentences with the correct term, making grammatical changes if necessary. You may use a word more than once.

Executive:

Execute:

President:

Presidential:

Preside:

1. Article II of the Federal Constitution vests federal _____ powers in the _____.

2. The president of the United States _____ over the _____ branch of government.

3. Voters throughout the United States elect the president every four years during the _____ election.

4. The function of the federal _____ is to_____ or carry out federal laws.

5. The defendant was convicted of murder and sentenced to the death penalty. The state _____ the person: the state government carried out the person's death.

The Structure of the Federal Executive

The President of the United States

Article II of the Federal Constitution vests executive powers in the president. The president is the head of the executive branch and serves a four-year term with the vice president of the United States.

Although Article II governs executive powers, Article I's legislative process specifies the president's role in the enactment of statutes. Read the following excerpt from the Constitution, Article I, Section 7. The portions in italics detail the president's role in enacting laws.

> *Every Bill which shall have passed the House of Representatives and the Senate, shall, before it becomes a Law, be presented to the President of the United States; If he approve he shall sign it, but if not he shall return it with his Objections* [called a *veto*] *to that House in which it shall have originated* [*for reconsideration*]. . . . If after such Reconsideration two thirds of that House shall agree to pass the Bill, it shall be sent, together with the Objections, to the other House, by which it shall likewise be reconsidered, and if approved by two thirds of that House, it shall become a Law. . . . *If any Bill shall not be returned by the President within ten days (Sundays excepted) after it shall have been presented to him, the Same shall be a Law, in like Manner as if he had signed it, unless the Congress by their Adjournment prevent its Return, in which Case it shall not be a law.*

If the president approves a bill, he signs it into law. If the president rejects or vetoes the bill, he sends it back to Congress. This process provides the president with a *check* on Congress's power to pass laws.

| **EXERCISE 26** | ## Constitutional Excerpts |

Instructions: Review the constitutional excerpts on the previous page, and then answer the following questions.

1. How many members of *both* houses of Congress must vote to override a president's veto?

2. If the president signs a bill, it becomes law. How can a bill become law without the president's signature?

3. Look back at the National Motor Vehicle Theft Act in the *Statutes at Large* in lesson 2.4. Did the president sign the bill into law, or did the bill become law without the president's signature?

The Cabinet and Federal Agencies

The executive branch does not consist only of the president and vice president alone, but this branch employs over four million people,[1] including members of the Cabinet and other executive-agency employees who carry out the laws.

The Cabinet

The Cabinet members are the fifteen most trusted presidential advisers (and others): the vice president and the head of each executive department in the following list. Federal agencies carry out the laws by investigating violations of law, and when permitted, creating rules governing vast subject matter such as protecting the borders (Homeland Security), ensuring food safety (Agriculture), health care (Health and Human Services), maintaining the military (Defense), and maintaining safe roads (Transportation). Here is a list of the fifteen executive departments:

1. Department of Agriculture
2. Department of Commerce
3. Department of Defense
4. Department of Education
5. Department of Energy
6. Department of Health and Human Services
7. Department of Homeland Security
8. Department of Housing and Urban Development
9. Department of the Interior

10. Department of Justice, led by the US Attorney General
11. Department of Labor
12. Department of State, led by the Secretary of State
13. Department of Transportation
14. Department of the Treasury
15. Department of Veterans Affairs

The heads of most departments are called a *secretary*, such as the *secretary of agriculture* and the *secretary of commerce*.

Secretary, in context: Read the following case title from the Obamacare decision from lesson 2.3. When that case began, Kathleen Sebelius was the head of Health and Human Services (no. 6, on the previous page), the administrative agency responsible for carrying out health care laws.

SUPREME COURT OF THE UNITED STATES
Syllabus

NATIONAL FEDERATION OF INDEPENDENT BUSINESS ET AL. *v.* SEBELIUS, SECRETARY OF HEALTH AND HUMAN SERVICES, ET AL.

Title of the case from the United States Supreme Court decision

The Department of Justice and the Attorney General

One of the president's Cabinet members is the attorney general (AG), who leads the Department of Justice (DOJ). The Department of Justice is vast, with over forty organizations including the Federal Bureau of Investigation (FBI, or the feds), which investigates violations of federal law and the United States attorneys, who represent the federal government in federal courts: "With a budget of approximately $25 billion, the DOJ is the world's largest law office and the central agency for the enforcement of federal laws."[2]

Some of the attorneys who work in the Department of Justice include

▸ *Attorney general (AG).* There is one attorney general for the federal government, appointed by the president of the United States. States each have their own attorneys general.

Question:
Which terms reveal that *United States attorneys* litigate federal and not state cases?

▸ *United States attorneys (USA).* The US attorneys represent the United States in civil and criminal cases in the federal courts. There is one head of each US attorney's office, called the United States attorney; the attorneys who work for the US attorneys in the ninety-four federal judicial districts throughout the United States are called assistant United States attorneys (AUSAs).

▸ *Solicitor general.* There is one solicitor general, who represents the United States before the United States Supreme Court.

WORD STUDY | *Nominate, Confirm, Appoint*

1. *To nominate* is to name or select a person for a particular position.
2. *To confirm* is to approve of that nomination.
3. *To appoint* is to officially place someone in a position, usually in an official ceremony.

The president of the United States (chief executive) *nominates* the attorney general, United States attorneys, the solicitor general, US Supreme Court justices, and others, and the Senate Committee on the Judiciary (in one house of the federal legislature) holds hearings to vet the candidate's qualifications. If the Senate *confirms* (approves) the nominee through a vote, the president then officially *appoints* the nominee to serve.

WORD STUDY | *Suffix -ee*

The suffix *-ee* may signify that a word describes a person who receives an action, as compared with a person acting. For instance, when the president acts to nominate federal officials, the person who receives the nomination is the *nominee*. When an employer is the person acting and hires someone for a job, the person who received the job is the *employee*. In these *-ee* words, the primary syllable stress is on the *ee* when speaking.

Two common words that end in *-ee* but do not mean "the recipient of an action" are *committee* and *coffee*.

▸ A *committee* (primary syllable stress on the *i*) is a group of people who meet together, such as the Senate Committee on the Judiciary, which vets the president's nominees. However, a *committee* (primary syllable stress on the *ee*) is a person who is committed to some place, such as a hospital.
▸ *Coffee* has primary syllable stress on the *o*.

EXERCISE 27 | Suffix -ee

Instructions: Fill in the blanks with the correct word from the word box, one per blank.

Word Box				
nominee	appointee	lessee	employee	appellee
grantee	assignee	covenantee	attendees	permittee

1. The president nominated a new United States attorney for the District of Massachusetts and is the president's _____.

2. After a successful confirmation hearing, the Fed chairman was appointed to serve on the Board of Governors. She is the newest Fed _____.

3. The business seller signed a covenant not to compete, agreeing with the buyer not to work in the state after selling the business. The buyer received the covenant and is the _____.

4. The mother assigned her interest in the home to her son. The son is the _____.

5. The employer conducted an interview and offered the lawyer a job. The lawyer is the law firm's newest _____.

6. The university received a large grant (money) from the federal government to conduct important scientific research. The university is the _____.

7. The lecture on the scope of Congress's commerce clause power was well attended. There were over one hundred _____.

8. A person who receives a permit to operate a restaurant in a city is called a _____ and may, when authorized by law, allow dog owners to sit in outdoor areas with their dogs.

9. The plaintiff lost the case and appealed. The defendant, who won the case and did not appeal, is the _____.

10. The woman leased the apartment from the owner-lessor. She is the _____.

Federal Administrative Agencies

Federal agencies regulate a vast number of areas.[3] The following are some examples of areas that these agencies regulate that are important to people and may affect their daily lives:

► The Federal Reserve (The Fed) regulates monetary policy such as certain interest rates (interest is money earned on invested money). The Fed had kept interest rates near zero for a number of recent years, and the Fed's decisions about when, and how much, to increase certain interest rates were repeatedly in the news.

► The Federal Communications Commission (FCC) regulates communications throughout the United States, such as by radio, cellular telephone, television, and the internet. One issue is *net neutrality*, which requires that internet providers be neutral, that is, give equal access to the internet without charging consumers for access to the World Wide Web.

► The Food and Drug Administration (FDA) is part of the Department of Health and Human Services (HHS) and regulates food safety and drugs, such as approval of new medicines. Two current HHS issues concern the regulation of genetically modified foods* and the regulation of health care.

* Some genetically modified salmon and crops are already being sold for consumption, where permitted.

► The Transportation Security Administration (TSA) and Immigration and Customs Enforcement (ICE) are two of the twenty-two agencies that are part of the Department of Homeland Security. Current issues concern immigration into the United States, cyber security, and border security with respect to people illegally crossing borders into the United States.[4]

► The Federal Aviation Administration (FAA) is part of the Department of Transportation and regulates air safety. One current issue concerns drone use.

Each of the subject areas that agencies regulate is quite specific in content and may require experts with specialized knowledge in order to create effective rules to protect people. For example, doctors may work at the FDA to effectively create rules about the safety of new drugs, as they have specialized knowledge in the medical field.

WORD STUDY | *Executive Terms*

Read the newspaper excerpts and the following descriptions. The italicized portions of the quotation refer to specific members and parts of the executive branch.

1. "*US* Renews Apple Fight": "*Federal prosecutors* pursue new court ruling to open iPhone in New York Drug Case. *The Justice Department* said on Friday it will seek a court order to force Apple Inc. to help unlock an iPhone seized as part of a New York drug investigation."

- *US* refers here to federal prosecutors within the Department of Justice.
- *Federal prosecutors* means United States attorneys.
- The *Justice Department* here includes federal prosecutors who work for the Department of Justice.

Source: Devlin Barrett, "US to Keep Pushing Apple to Unlock iPhone in New York Case," *Wall Street Journal*, April 9–10, 2017, 1.

To fire here means to remove someone from a job.

2. "President Trump fired* [Sally Q. Yates, the *acting attorney general*] after she defiantly refused to defend his executive order closing the nation's borders to refugees and people from predominantly Muslim countries."

- The *acting attorney general* refers to the then attorney general, the head of the Department of Justice. The AG was only "acting" because she was in the position temporarily, until the new president nominated an AG under his new administration and the Senate confirmed the new AG.

Source: Michael D. Shear, Mark Landler, Matt Apuzzo and Eric Lichtblau, "Trump Fires [Sally Q. Yates] Who Defied Him," *New York Times*, January 30, 2017, A1.

3. "Julian Castro *the HUD secretary*, is expected . . . to announce guidance that details his agency's interpretation of how the fair housing law applies to policies that exclude people with criminal records, a group that is not explicitly protected by the act but falls under it in certain circumstances. Federal officials said landlords must distinguish between arrests and convictions and cannot use an arrest to ban applicants."

- *HUD secretary* refers to a member of the President's cabinet, the head of a federal administrative agency abbreviated *HUD* (Department of Housing and Urban Development)

Source: Mireya Navarro, "Federal Housing Officials Warn Against Blanket Bans of Ex-Offenders," *New York Times*, April 4, 2016, A14.

4. "*US safety regulators* have decided not to seek a recall after investigating complaints the door ajar warning lights won't turn off on thousands of Ford SUVs. The probe began in September and found nearly 2,700 complaints and over 33,000 warranty claims due to the problem with the 2011 to 2013 [Ford cars]. The complaints included 14 drivers who said doors had opened unexpectedly. . . . But the National Highway Traffic Safety Administration determined the doors were either opened by the passengers or were not latched properly. The agency found no unreasonable safety risk."

- *US safety regulators* refers to the National Highway Traffic Safety Administration, an agency that regulates (carries out) policy relating to car safety.

Source: Associated Press, "Feds Close Probe of Ford SUV Door Ajar Lights without Recall," *Washington Post*, March 24, 2017, www.washingtonpost.com.

5. "Preet Bahara, one of the most high-profile *federal prosecutors* in the country, said he was fired . . . after refusing to submit a letter of resignation [to the new Trump administration]."

- *Federal prosecutor* here refers to the former United States Attorney for the Southern District of New York, the lead prosecutor in the district.

Source: Devlin Barrett, Sari Horwitz, and Robert Costa, "New York Federal Prosecutor Preet Bahara Says He Was Fired by Trump Administration," *Washington Post*, March 11, 2017, www.washingtonpost.com.

6. "*US* Arrests 39 Members of MS-13, Gang Blamed for Long Island Killings": "Thirty-nine members of MS-13, a brutal gang with roots in Central America, were arrested by the *immigration authorities* in New York in the past month, officials said on Wednesday."

   - Here, *US* refers to federal immigration agents (authorities) from agencies that carry out immigration laws by arresting people who are in the United States illegally. *Immigration authorities* include members of the agency called the Immigration and Customs Enforcement (commonly called "ICE") and members of the Department of Homeland Security.

   Source: Sarah Maslin Nir and Arielle Dollinger, "US Arrests 39 Members of MS-13, Gang Blamed for Long Island Killings," *New York Times*, June 15, 2017, A23.

LESSON 3.3 The Powers of the Federal Executive

Article II includes the following references to federal executive powers:

Section 1

The executive power shall be vested in a President of the United States of America. . . .

Before he Enter on the Execution of his office he shall take the following Oath or Affirmation:—"I do solemnly swear (or affirm) that I will faithfully execute the Office of the President of the United States, and will to the best of my Ability, preserve, protect and defend the Constitution of the United States."

Section 2

The President shall be Commander in Chief of the Army and Navy of the United States. . . . He shall have Power to grant Reprieves and Pardons for Offenses against the United States, except in Cases of Impeachment.

He shall have Power, by and with the Advice and Consent of the Senate, to make Treaties, provided two thirds of the Senators present concur; and he shall nominate, and by and with the Advice and Consent of the Senate, shall appoint Ambassadors, other public Ministers and Consuls, Judges of the supreme Court, and all other Officers of the United States, whose Appointments are not herein otherwise provided for, and which shall be established by Law.

Section 3

[The President] shall take Care that the Laws be faithfully executed.

The Constitution vests "executive power" in the president and grants the express power to pardon (forgive) people who commit federal crimes. Also, with the Senate's approval, the president can make treaties and appoint certain public officials, including ambassadors and US Supreme Court judges and other federal judges.

WORD STUDY | *Treaties, Treatises*

Article II, § 2, authorizes the president to make treaties, with the Senate's approval.

Treaties are agreements between foreign nations, such as the Treaty of Versailles, ending World War I. *Treatises* are scholarly books that summarize specific, often legal, topics.

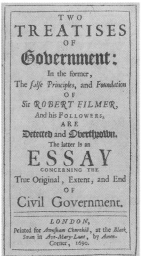

Treaties: agreements between countries

Treatises: scholarly books

The Federal Executive's Source of Law

The President

The president can issue proclamations and executive orders. Proclamations[5] are sometimes ceremonial, such as President Lincoln's 1863 proclamation proclaiming the fourth Thursday of every November to be the Thanksgiving holiday.[6] One famous presidential proclamation was President Lincoln's 1863 Emancipation Proclamation, which related to efforts to free slaves. Most recently, President Trump issued a controversial proclamation concerning immigration, affecting who can enter the United States.[7]

Executive orders are signed presidential statements that can direct agencies to act or carry out the laws: "An executive order is not the president creating new law or appropriating new money from the US Treasury—both things that are the domain of Congress; it is the president instructing the government how it is to work within the parameters that are already set by Congress and the Constitution."[8]

The *power of the pen* refers to the president's power to vastly affect the law with one signature with a pen. For example, on January 20, 2017, President Trump's first day in office, he issued an executive order, excerpted on the following page, that in effect directed the Department of Health and Human Services, the agency that administers or carries out health care, to reduce spending on Obamacare. Using the *power of the pen*, the president vastly affected the reach of this law. This executive order had reportedly resulted in the reduction in the amount of money that the Department of Health and Human Services (HHS) has spent advertising Obamacare coverage, resulting in fewer people obtaining health care coverage;[9] the act's intended purpose was the opposite: to expand health insurance throughout the nation.

Executive Order Minimizing the Economic Burden of the Patient Protection and Affordable Care Act Pending Repeal[10]

By the authority vested in me as President by the Constitution and the laws of the United States of America, it is hereby ordered as follows:

Section 1. It is the policy of my Administration to seek the prompt repeal of the Patient Protection and Affordable Care Act (Public Law 111-148), as amended (the "Act"). In the meantime, pending such repeal, it is imperative for the executive branch to ensure that the law is being efficiently implemented, take all actions consistent with law to minimize the unwarranted economic and regulatory burdens of the Act. . . .

Sec. 2. To the maximum extent permitted by law, the Secretary of Health and Human Services (Secretary) and the heads of all other executive departments and agencies (agencies) with authorities and responsibilities under the Act shall exercise all authority and discretion available to them to waive, defer, grant exemptions from, or delay the implementation of any provision or requirement of the Act that would impose a fiscal burden on any State or a cost, fee, tax, penalty, or regulatory burden on individuals, families, healthcare providers, health insurers, patients, recipients of health-care services, purchasers of health insurance, or makers of medical devices, products, or medications.

Notice that the title of this executive order ends with the words "pending repeal." This statement reflects Republicans' desire and efforts to repeal Obamacare in Congress in 2017, efforts that were pending and under consideration at the time the president signed this executive order.

WORD STUDY | *Ban*

To *ban* means to prohibit something.

If a professor *bans* all laptops from class, students are prohibited from bringing computers to class; instead they must take handwritten notes.

An executive order can result in a *ban* on certain actions. For example, on January 27, 2017, President Trump issued an executive order, colloquially called a "travel ban," that briefly resulted in a ban (prohibition) on people from certain countries from entering the United States. The president claimed that the travel ban's purpose was to "Protect[] the Nation from Foreign Terrorist Entry Into the United States."[11] A later executive order and proclamation (travel ban) were the subject of litigation by people who claimed that the ban was unconstitutional and have been a source of extensive debate and litigation.

| *Blanket Ban*

A blanket ban on nonservice pets would cover all pets that are not service animals.

A *blanket ban* means a *total* ban or prohibition. A blanket of snow entirely covers the grass; a blanket for sleeping entirely covers a bed; a blanket ban entirely covers a specified act.

Example 1: President Trump issued an executive order temporarily ordering a ban on foreign nationals from seven countries from entering the United States. A later, revised executive order removed the *blanket ban* on all Iraqi citizens entering the United States.

Example 2: Some building owners (landlords) who rent apartments refuse to rent their apartments to people who have committed crimes. Julian Castro, former secretary of the agency carrying out housing laws (the Department of Housing and Urban Development, HUD), reportedly concluded that *blanket bans* on renting to people both arrested for and convicted of crimes could violate the law (the Fair Housing Act).[12]

Example 3: After tragic shootings throughout the United States, people throughout the United States have been venting anger at the lack of strong gun laws by protesting and demanding that legislators enact stricter gun control laws. In Parkland, Florida, a former student with a military-style assault rifle killed seventeen people, including teachers and teenage students. Students and others protested in the Florida state capital, and legislators swiftly passed some new gun control laws, signed into law by Florida's governor. One of the laws is a *blanket ban* on sale of guns to any person under twenty-one years of age, thus raising the minimum age for buying guns from eighteen to twenty-one, as the statute prescribes.[13]

Federal Agencies

Rules and regulations from federal agencies are an important source of law. "Agencies create regulations (also known as 'rules') under the authority of Congress to help government carry out public policy."[14] Recall that *carrying out* the laws is a traditional executive power, *legislating* is a traditional legislative power, and *adjudicating* is a traditional judicial power. Yet Article I, Article II, and Article III of the Federal Constitution create only the three branches of the federal government and do not create agencies; Congress can create certain federal agencies and define their powers to carry out laws, create rules and regulations, and, under some certain, adjudicate violation of the rules at hearings, in which an *administrative law judge* presides. These agencies act under the authority of Congress and can only promulgate rules and regulations (called *rulemaking* power) if Congress authorized that agency to do so.

Federal agency regulations are printed in the *Federal Register* and the *Code of Federal Regulations* (C.F.R.).[15] Title 42 of the United States Code contains federal statutes related to health care, including PPACA, or Obamacare, previously discussed in lesson 2.3, and 42 C.F.R. contains Department of Health and Human Services agency rules implementing certain provisions of health law.

Under Obamacare, most Americans were required to have certain health insurance coverage or pay what is called a *shared responsibility* payment or penalty.[16] This mandated that a nonexempt taxpayer without such coverage pay a monetary penalty.

The statutory rule prescribing the individual mandate is 26 U.S.C. § 5000A. This is not 42 U.S.C., related to health care, but 26 U.S.C., related to the subject of taxes. 26 C.F.R. contains rules and regulations governing the payment and collection of federal taxes. The federal agency responsible for collecting income taxes created rules for collecting the shared responsibility payment, and when filing federal tax returns, taxpayers had to state whether or not they had the required health care coverage or were exempt from the requirement. With exceptions, those without the required coverage had to pay the shared responsibility payment to the US government. Ultimately, in 2017, though Congress did not repeal Obamacare, it did eliminate this penalty when enacting a federal tax law, the Tax Cuts and Jobs Act of 2017, P.L. No. 115-97, 131 Stat. 2054.

WORD STUDY | *Red tape, Promulgate, Suffix -gate*

Red tape refers to strict and excessive numbers of regulations and requirements, usually resulting in negative consequences. *Red tape* in the form of FAA regulations negatively affected Amazon's "Prime Air" efforts to deliver its commercial merchandise by drone.[17]

Promulgate has a similar meaning to *enact*, or to officially become law. *Promulgate* often refers to rules and regulations from agencies. Agencies *promulgate* rules and regulations, and Congress *promulgates* (or enacts) statutes.

In some circumstances (not applicable to the term *promulgate*), combining a word with *-gate* came to mean "controversy" or "scandal" after a 1972 event called *Watergate*, which occurred during President Nixon's presidency. Members of the Republican Party who were working for President Nixon broke into the Democratic Party headquarters in a Washington, DC, hotel called the Watergate Hotel to get secret information about the Democratic Party.* The break-in came to be known as *Watergate*, and the suffix *-gate* came to describe a controversy or scandal.

* In *United States v. Nixon*, 418 U.S. 683 (1974), the US Supreme Court ruled that President Nixon had to turn over certain subpoenaed recordings for Watergate-related criminal prosecutions.

Here are some other recent *-gates*:

Deflategate was a scandal in which a professional football player was accused of deflating (taking the air out of) a football so that it was easier to catch during a football game, resulting in a win.

Hoodiegate was a controversy when Mark Zuckerberg, the Facebook founder, wore an informal sweatshirt with a hood (called a *hoodie*) to the stock exchange on Wall Street in New York City when Facebook became a publicly traded company. Some people viewed such casual dress as disrespectful.

Bridgegate was a scandal in which members of the Republican New Jersey governor Chris Christie's office closed one lane of a major crossing between New York and New Jersey called the George Washington Bridge. This closing resulted in major traffic problems and hours of delays to emergency vehicles, school buses, and other drivers who were stuck on the bridge. Members of Governor Christie's staff claimed that the closure was for a "traffic study." But in fact, these staffers were convicted of crimes related to the closure. Federal prosecutors (US attorneys who tried the case in a federal district court in New Jersey) proved to a jury that the Christie staffers closed the bridge because the Democratic mayor of the New Jersey city located at one end of the bridge refused to support Governor Christie in his reelection campaign. This is *partisanship* to an extreme.

Envelopegate was a controversy that occurred at the 2017 Oscars Awards ceremony. The accounting firm responsible for handing out the envelopes containing the winners' names gave the wrong envelope to Faye Dunaway and Warren Beatty, who announced that *La La Land* won the award for best picture, when *Moonlight* had actually won the award.

But not every word ending with *-gate* means "scandal." *Promulgate* does not refer to a scandal, even though it ends in *-gate*.

WORD STUDY | *Overreach*

Overreach means to act over or beyond one's powers, in effect reaching over other branches to exercise unauthorized power.

Executive Overreach
Under the US system, each branch of government has specific constitutional powers, and Article I, § 1, vests legislative powers in Congress and not the executive. The president can *overreach* when purportedly acting beyond his or her powers.[18]

Ultimately, if a person or other entity such as a business or a state challenges an executive action in court, the court would decide if the executive overreached in violation of the separation of powers or if these orders are within the scope of the executive's authority.*

* San Francisco v. Trump, 897 F.3d 1225 (9th Cir. 2018), struck down President Trump's executive order directing agencies to withhold certain federal grant money, without congressional authorization, from sanctuary jurisdictions.

Prosecutorial Overreach

Prosecutors can *overreach* when they bring criminal charges against people that may go over or beyond the original scope of the law enacted by Congress. Enron was a Texas corporation involved in a major scandal involving fraud, during which the company's accounting firm shredded (cut up into small pieces) documents in order to destroy evidence of the fraud. After Enron, Congress enacted the Sarbanes-Oxley Act of 2002, 116 Stat. 745, under which 18 U.S.C., § 1519, made it a crime, under certain circumstances, "to destroy[] . . . any record, document or tangible object."

Prosecutors charged a fisherman, John Yates, with violating § 1519 by destroying a tangible object: fish. Federal agents boarded Yates's fishing boat and found fish that were smaller than the size that federal regulations allow fishermen to catch. When Yates brought the boat back to shore, the undersized fish were not on the boat, and prosecutors filed charges against Yates for destroying the fish, which prosecutors alleged were "tangible object[s]" within the meaning of 18 U.S.C., § 1519. Yates was convicted at trial, but ultimately the United States Supreme Court decided that fish are not "tangible objects" within the meaning of a statute that criminalizes destroying documents and other records and objects (but not fish). *Yates v. United States*, 574 U.S. ____ , 135 S. Ct. 1074 (2015). *Yates* could be an example of prosecutorial *overreach* because prosecutors went beyond what Congress contemplated when enacting 18 U.S.C., § 1519, when they charged Yates with a violation of this statute.*

Shredding a document

* In *Yates*, four US Supreme Court justices dissented, concluding that fish were "tangible objects" within the meaning of this statute.

EXERCISE 28 | # Federal, State, or Local: Who Executes the Law?

Background: The executive branches of the federal, state, and local governments execute, or carry out, laws. There may be several sets of rules that people must follow, which come from agencies on the federal, state, and local levels.

	Federal	State	Local
Head of the executive branch (chief executive)	President of the United States (elected)	Governor (elected)	Mayor (city) (elected) (others exist)
Lead attorney	Head of the Department of Justice, the attorney general (appointed)	State attorney general (one AG in each of the individual fifty states) (elected or appointed)	District attorney (elected or appointed)
Attorneys	Attorney General's Office United States attorneys (in the ninety-four judicial districts)[19]	State Attorney General's Office	Varies, for example the New York City corporation counsel (civil), district attorney (criminal)
Agencies	Federal agencies	State agencies	Local agencies

Instructions: Write whether the following describe a federal, state, or local executive branch member. The first one is completed as a model.

1. United States attorney for the Eastern District of New York: part of the federal executive (prosecutor in federal cases)

2. Governor of Texas:

3. Mayor of Chicago, Illinois:

4. Los Angeles district attorney:

5. Town attorney for the town of Islip, New York:

6. New York State attorney general:

7. The United States solicitor general:

8. Secretary of the Department of Health and Human Services:

9. The commissioner (head) of the New York administrative agency called the Department of Health, administering health issues in New York State, such as regulating the use of e-cigarettes:

10. New York City Department of Health, which issues birth and death certificates for people who are born or die within New York City:

Unit 3 Review

Instructions: Fill in the blanks with the correct word from the word box, making any necessary grammatical changes. You may use a term more than once.

Word Box		
Execute	Executive	Promulgate

Article II of the United States Constitution establishes the largest of the three federal branches of government, the _____ branch of government, employing over four million people. The president heads this branch, which _____, enforces or carries out, the laws. One way that the president carries out the laws is by appointing the Cabinet members, including the heads of agencies, called secretaries, the attorney general, and United States attorneys in the different federal districts. US attorneys prosecute criminal cases in the federal courts and defend the government in civil cases. The president can issue _____ orders and can direct agencies to carry out the law.

Administrative agencies are part of the _____ branch. Agency members may have specialized knowledge of specific subject areas in order to effectively _____ (carry out) laws as authorized by Congress, such as regulations from certain administrative agencies including the Food and Drug Administration (FDA). Congress must affirmatively grant an agency the power to _____ regulations.

UNIT 4   The Federal Judiciary

LESSON 4.1 The Constitutional Authority for the Federal Judiciary

Article III, §1, of the United States Constitution vests federal judicial powers as follows:

> The judicial Power of the United States shall be vested in one supreme Court, and in such inferior Courts as the Congress may from time to time ordain and establish.

The western entrance to the United States Supreme Court Building in Washington, DC.

On the top of the eastern side of the United States Supreme Court Building, there are relief statues of (*from left to right*) Confucius, Moses, and Solon, historical lawgivers from Eastern civilizations.

EXERCISE 29 | Word Forms

Instructions: Define the following terms and write the word's part of speech, either noun, adjective, or verb. Then fill in the blanks in the following sentences with the correct term, making grammatical changes if necessary. You may use a word more than once.

Judiciary:

Judicial:

Justice:

To adjudicate:

Judge:

To adjudge:

To vest:

To vet:

1. Article III of the Federal Constitution _____ the _____ power in the federal _____ .

2. The Senate holds hearings to _____ the qualifications of US Supreme Court _____ to determine their qualifications to serve in the _____ branch.

3. The federal _____ consists of the United States Supreme Court and courts inferior (lower) than the Supreme Court. The Federal Constitution _____ power to create these lower courts in Congress.

4. Judges _____ legal issues in court cases.

5. The defendant was _____ guilty of committing multiple crimes.

6. A _____ can serve in either a trial court or an appellate court.

LESSON 4.2 The Structure of the Federal Judiciary

Article III Courts

* The official name
is *Supreme Court of
the United States,*
and the court is also
referred to as the
US Supreme Court.

Federal courts created under Article III of the Federal Constitution are called *Article III courts.* Federal court judges who are appointed by the president and serve in an Article III court are called *Article III judges.*

The federal judiciary consists of one Supreme Court* and those courts inferior to (lower than) the US Supreme Court that Congress establishes.[1] *Lower than* means below the Supreme Court in position, as illustrated in the following chart. A higher court has authority to review and change a lower court's decision.

Cases from state high courts: The US Supreme Court can review state court decisions interpreting federal law

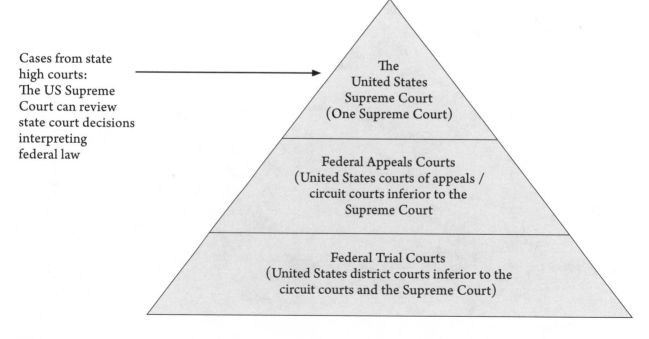

The United States Supreme Court (One Supreme Court)

Federal Appeals Courts (United States courts of appeals / circuit courts inferior to the Supreme Court

Federal Trial Courts (United States district courts inferior to the circuit courts and the Supreme Court)

The *United States Supreme Court* means only the highest court in the federal court system. However, the *Supreme Court* (without *United States*) may mean an entirely different court. In New York, lower trial courts are named *Supreme Court*.

In the following chart, the arrow on the left illustrates the path of a case, beginning in a federal trial (lower) court and continuing with review by a higher court. The losing party can appeal (seek review of) a decision from a lower, inferior court to a higher court.

Number of courts and location	Structure and description (see the federal courtroom setup illustration on the following page)	Minimum number of votes to win
There is only one *US Supreme Court*, located in Washington, DC	Nine justices together review a single case from the lower courts (though a vacancy or recusal could result in fewer than nine justices hearing a case). Only the lawyers argue the case to the justices. There is no witness testimony and no jury.	A majority—at least five of the nine justices.
Federal appeals courts are also called *circuit courts* and are divided into thirteen *circuits* located throughout the United States.	Three judges together review a single case from the lower trial courts. Only the lawyers argue the case to the judges. There is no witness testimony and no jury.	A majority—at least two of the three judges. The three judges who preside over an appeal are, together, called a *panel*. After the panel issues a decision, the losing party can request that all of the appellate judges review a decision. This review, which is rarely granted, is called an *en banc* review by a larger panel of appellate judges.
Federal trial courts are called *federal district courts* and are divided into ninety-four districts (geographic areas) located throughout the United States.	One judge presides over the trial of a single case. If the parties choose not to have a jury trial, the judge decides who wins; this is called a *bench* trial.	Bench trial: one judge decides who wins; jury trial: number of jurors and minimum vote to win varies by type of case and jurisdiction.

A party in a federal court *may* have the opportunity to have

1. a trial in a federal trial (district) court;
2. a review of the trial court decision by an intermediate federal appeals (circuit) court; and
3. a review of the circuit court decision by the United States Supreme Court.

The following pages describe each of these court levels in more detail.

Typical Federal Courtrooms Setup

The High Court
One United States Supreme Court

No jury, no witnesses

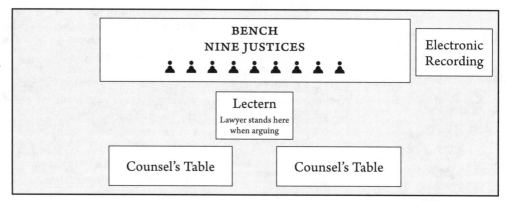

Intermediate Federal Appeals Courts
Thirteen circuits

No jury, no witnesses

Higher courts review the *record* from the trial court

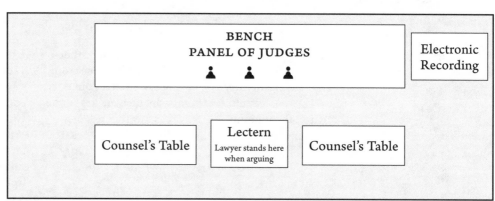

Federal Trial Courts
Ninety-four federal judicial districts

Notice that only the trial court has a *witness stand* and a *jury box*

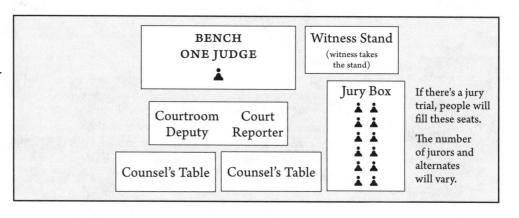

Federal Trial Courts (District Courts)

Recall from unit 1 that the terms *federal* and *United States* may be synonyms. US district courts are trial courts in the federal court system.

Federal courts within each state are divided into one or more geographic areas, called a federal *district*. There are ninety-four separate districts throughout the entire United States. Therefore, with fifty states in total, some states have more than one federal judicial district within one state.

WORD STUDY | *Terminology from Trial Courts*

Civil here does not have the same meaning as *civil* in the context of a non-common-law, civil code country. It means a case that does not involve the violation of a criminal law.

Criminal Case	Civil Case
A person allegedly commits a crime (*breaks the law*)	Noncriminal, resolving issues between two parties, such as • a car accident • a contract dispute
Result: Jail or other sentence if convicted	Result: Monetary relief (damages/money) if found liable Nonmonetary relief (such as an injunction to do or stop doing something)

WORD STUDY | *People in a Case: Party (Singular), Parties (Plural), Adversary, Advocate, Plaintiff, Defendant, Petitioner, Respondent, Appellant, Appellee; Sue, Suit; Prosecute, Prosecution*

* An *advocate* works for people; an *adversary* works against them.

The *parties* in both civil and criminal cases are *adversaries* (opponents). An *adversary* is an *opponent*, but an *advocate** is a *proponent*, or someone who stands up for another person. Attorneys are advocates for their clients, and there are other advocates who are not attorneys. Helen Keller was an advocate, seeking positive change for deaf and blind individuals (see the photo of her statue in lesson 2.4).

Plaintiff	against (v.)	Defendant
The parties are *adversaries* or *opponents* (*v.* is short for *versus* or against)		
The person or entity (such as a business or a state) commencing an action		The person whom the plaintiff is suing or, in a criminal case, the person whom prosecutors have charged with a crime, both called the *defendant*
Plaintiff in a civil case, who *sues* or *brings suit*		
Prosecutors in a criminal case, bring or file charges in a criminal case in the name of the government		

Petitioner	against (v.)	Respondent
A person commencing an action with a petition seeking certain types of nonmonetary relief		The person responding to the petition
Civil: injunction, mandamus, and others		
Criminal: habeas corpus and others		

Appellant	against (v.)	Appellee (also respondent)
The losing party in the court below who appeals and seeks higher court review claiming there was an error in the trial court		The winning party in the court below

To sue (verb) means to commence a civil case in court. One party *sues* another party, commencing an action. *Suit* is a noun related to the verb *to sue*.

To prosecute (verb) means to commence or litigate a criminal case. Compare the verb *to persecute*, with a very different meaning from *prosecute*. To persecute means to target and mistreat a person for his or her beliefs.

Prosecution has two meanings: (1) the people who litigate criminal cases (generally United States attorneys in federal cases, attorneys general in certain statewide cases, and district attorneys in local counties, individually called prosecutors); and (2) the process of litigating a criminal case (such as a criminal prosecution).

WORD STUDY | *Types of Trials: Bench Trial and Jury Trial*

The parties in both civil and criminal cases decide which type of trial to have. The rules governing juries and whether the parties must agree to the type of trial vary by jurisdiction.

Bench trial	Jury trial
There is no jury; the judge hears the evidence and decides which party wins. In criminal cases, a defendant may prefer a bench trial when charged with a crime evoking strong emotions.	A jury, consisting of people from the community, hears the evidence. A judge presides over the trial, but if a case reaches the jury, the jury ultimately decides who wins.

Attorneys' opening statements

Witnesses testify

Evidence submitted

Attorneys' closing statements

Jury charge (in a jury trial, the judge's instructions to jurors)

Jury trial: the jury deliberates, decides who wins

Bench trial: the trial judge decides who wins

Jury charge

Examples of a trial judge's instructions to the jury:

- the elements of a civil or criminal statute or common law cause of action that the party with the burden of proof must prove
- which party has the burden of proof
- what is the standard of proof

Witnesses *take the stand* at trial, answering the lawyers' questions (testifying) at trials. Compare the expression *taking a stand*, which means taking a position on an issue.

Take *the* stand	Take *a* stand
The witness *taking the stand* (testifying at trial). The *stand* is short for *witness stand*, where the witness sits when testifying.	People *taking a stand* (taking a position) on an issue by protesting.

WORD STUDY | *Trial and Related Terms: To Litigate, Litigation, Litigious, Litigant, Litigator; To Try, Trial*

To litigate (verb) means to resolve disputes through the courts, including but not limited to the actual trial of a case. *Litigation* (noun) is the act of litigating, or resolving disputes through the courts. Litigation involves many aspects of dispute resolution in courts, such as motion practice, trying cases, and arguing appeals.

▶ Lawyers *litigate* both civil and criminal cases.
▶ *Litigious* means, in effect, many lawsuits: in a *litigious* society, people sue each other often, bringing many civil cases in court.
▶ *Litigant* can mean either a plaintiff or prosecution or a defendant separately, or in the plural, *litigants* means both parties, the plaintiff and the defendant together.
▶ A *litigator* is an attorney who specializes in litigating cases in courts.*

* *Litigants* are the parties in a court case. *Litigators* are the attorneys who represent them.

To try (verb) in this context relates to the noun *trial*. Attorneys *try* cases during a trial in criminal and civil cases by presenting evidence such as witness testimony, photographs, videos, and documents in order to prove that their client should win.

Trials take place *only in trial courts*, where one judge presides. Many federal cases, both civil and criminal, are filed in the federal district courts; but in reality, there are far fewer actual trials, and both civil and criminal cases end before trials take place. According to the Federal Judicial Center, in the fiscal year ending 2017, approximately 290,000 civil cases and 75,000 criminal cases were filed in the US district courts.[2] Of these civil cases, only around 2,600 reached a trial; in criminal cases, during this period, over 67,000 defendants pleaded guilty, and 1,874 reached a trial (276 defendants acquitted and 1,598 defendants convicted).[3]

WORD STUDY | *Relief, Remedy*

Relief is the specific award that a party requests in a complaint or petition when filing a civil suit. These awards are also called remedies because a party is asking the court to remedy, or solve, a problem by giving the "relief sought" in the complaint or petition. Parties may seek monetary relief when they suffer certain types of injuries or nonmonetary relief when they will not be satisfied or adequately compensated by a monetary award.

A person whose land is being polluted by a neighboring corporation could seek a remedy that would order the corporation to stop polluting; a person adversely affected by a law could seek a judgment declaring the statute unconstitutional because money would be insufficient to redress or repair these injuries. Typical civil remedies are listed here:

Monetary Relief

1. Damages	General meaning in this context is a term of art meaning *compensation* or money.
2. Liquidated damages	A set or agreed-on term on the amount of damages. An example is in the sale of real property, when the parties agree that a buyer who breaches the contract (does not purchase the property) loses his or her 10 percent deposit (or another amount) that the contract specifies.
3. Treble damages	Triple the amount of damages, when authorized by statute.
4. Compensatory damages	"Money . . . [to pay for a] for loss or injury." *Black's Law Dictionary* (10th ed., 2014). These are designed to *compensate* an individual for actual losses or to make the person *whole*.
5. Punitive (exemplary) damages	"Damages awarded in addition to actual damages when the defendant acted with recklessness, malice, or deceit; specif., damages assessed by way of penalizing the wrongdoer, . . . making an example to others, . . . [and] deter[ring] blameworthy conduct." *Black's Law Dictionary* (10th ed., 2014). *Punitive*: to punish. *Exemplary*: to make an example of.
6. Economic damages Noneconomic damages	Economic: money damages that can easily be measured, such as lost wages or medical expenses. Noneconomic: money damages that are difficult to measure, such as emotional distress suffered as a bystander or loss of consortium, such as loss of a spouse's companionship.

Nonmonetary Relief

1. Writ	A general meaning: written orders, which take a variety of forms.
2. Mandamus	"Latin 'we command.' A [type of] writ issued by a court to compel performance of a particular act by a lower court or a governmental officer or body, usually to correct a prior action or failure to act." *Black's Law Dictionary* (10th ed., 2014).
3. Injunction	A court order that requires a person to do something (such as return property) or stop doing something (such as polluting or destroying property).*
4. Specific performance of a contract	"The court orders a party to actually perform its [contractual] promise as closely as possible, because monetary damages are somehow inadequate to fix the harm. Most commonly ordered in cases involving real property and rare chattels." *Wex Legal Dictionary*, www.law.cornell.edu/wex/.
5. Declaratory judgment	To declare something, such as a person being the true owner of property or a statute being unconstitutional. "A binding judgment from a court defining the legal relationship between parties and their rights in the matter before the court." *Wex Law Dictionary*, www.law.cornell.edu/wex/.

* *Enjoin* in this context means to stop, and *compel* means to require or mandate. An injunction may enjoin persons or entities from acting or compel them to act.

WORD STUDY | *Comparing Terminology in Civil and Criminal Cases*

Here are selected general explanations comparing terminology in civil and criminal cases.

	Civil case	Criminal case
Background	A person or entity suffers a monetary loss or seeks a court's powers to redress (give a remedy for) another type of injury for nonmonetary relief. Two examples of nonmonetary remedies are 1. an injunction, which is a court order to do or stop doing something (such as return property or not compete with a former employer); and 2. a declaratory judgment declaring a statute unconstitutional or constitutional (as in the Obamacare United States Supreme Court decision).	A person or another entity such as a corporation *breaks the law* (commits a crime). The feds (in federal cases) investigate violations of federal criminal laws. The state, local police or sheriffs investigate violations of state criminal laws. *Criminal* and *lawbreaker* are general terms that can mean a person who commits a crime. *Crook* is a colloquial term for a criminal. Specific terms applicable to one type of crime: *murderer* or *killer* (kills another person), *robber* (forcibly steals property), *burglar* (enters or stays unlawfully in a home or other structure to commit a crime such as stealing), *arsonist* (causes a fire), *stalker* (stalks or follows a person compulsively and without permission), and a *cyber thief* (steals material through a computer connection).

	Civil case	Criminal case
Parties: *v.* in case names is an abbreviation for *versus*, meaning "against"	*Plaintiff v. Defendant* A plaintiff begins a civil case. Common terms are - The plaintiff *sued, filed suit, filed a lawsuit,* or *brought suit.* - A defendant defends against the plaintiff's claims.	*Prosecution v. Defendant* The prosecution brings or files criminal charges against a criminal defendant. Verb: *to charge* ("The prosecution charged the defendant with violating 18 U.S.C. § 408.") In a criminal case, the title will include "The United States" in federal cases, e.g., *United States v. McBoyle,* or a state name in state cases, e.g., *People of the State of New York v. Jones, Commonwealth of Massachusetts v. Smith.*
Early termination: An agreement that ends a civil or criminal case, usually before a trial but can occur during trial as well	*Settle* The parties agree to terminate or settle a case before trial.	*Take a plea* (plea bargain); past tense: "The defendant *took a plea.*" The parties agree that the defendant may plead guilty to crimes resulting in a less severe sentence (i.e., less time in jail) than for the original crime(s) charged. The presiding judge must approve of the plea after an *allocution* (questioning), to be sure the defendant admits to the crime and understands the consequences of the plea.
Papers that a lawyer or prosecutor prepares	*Pleadings in civil actions* *Service of process* is delivery (by methods that statutes allow) of specific legal papers to give a defendant notice of the proceedings. A *summons* commands a person to answer a complaint. A civil *complaint* includes specific allegations of fact supporting the claim, the legal basis for the claim (e.g., negligence, breach of contract) and the relief sought. The defendant files an *answer* and can file a counterclaim, in a complaint against the plaintiff.	*Pleadings in criminal actions* A *criminal complaint*: lists initial criminal charges against a defendant. An *information*: in misdemeanors, which are crimes punishable by up to one year in jail. An *indictment*: in felonies, crimes punishable by more than one year in jail. In felonies, a grand jury (twelve to twenty-three people) hear evidence in secret with only the prosecutor present and the witness testifying. A grand jury may *indict* a defendant or defendants (issue a document called an *indictment* listing the crimes charged). A grand jury votes whether to indict before a trial; a trial (petit) jury hears evidence at trial and decides whether to convict. A criminal defendant does not file a responsive pleading (comparable to the *answer* in a civil case), instead pleading either guilty or not guilty in court at a stage called an *arraignment.*
Standard of proof (how much evidence)	Preponderance of the evidence Clear and convincing evidence	Proof beyond a reasonable doubt
Burden of proof (who must prove the case)	The plaintiff has the *burden of proof.* (For counterclaims by defendant against the plaintiff, the defendant has the *burden of proof.*)	The prosecution has the *burden of proof.*

	Civil case	Criminal case
Verdict (finding after trial by a judge in a bench trial or a jury in a jury trial)	Liable (civilly responsible) or not liable (Compare *libel*, which is a specific type of action in which a person seeks damages when another person makes false statements about him or her.)	*Guilty* (criminally responsible) or *not guilty* Convicts the defendant: *guilty* Acquits the defendant: *not guilty* Idioms: • *off the hook*: "The defendant was *off the hook* after the jury acquitted her." • *locked up* and *got*: "The judge locked the defendant up for 20 years" and "The defendant *got* 20 years" both mean that a judge sentenced a defendant to jail for twenty years.

EXERCISE 30 | Civil or Criminal Case?

Instructions: Decide whether each of the sentences describes a civil case or a criminal case or could describe both, and write "CI" (civil), "CR" (criminal), or "CI/CR" (both) in the blank. Then decide if the sentence could describe a state case, a federal case, or both, and write "S" (state) "F" (federal) or "S/F" (both) in the blank:

1. The defendant was prosecuted for violating N.Y. Penal Law § 120.00(1) __CR__

2. The plaintiff sued for libel. __CI__

3. The defense claims that prosecution did not meet the burden of proof. __CR / CI__

4. The defendant objected to the admissibility of the expert testimony. __CR/CI__

5. The plaintiff brought suit for breach of contract. __CI__

6. The jury found that the plaintiff was liable. __CI__

7. The jury returned a not guilty verdict, acquitting the defendant. __CR__

8. The district attorney charged the defendant with a violation of N.Y. Vehicle and Traffic Law § 1192. __CR__

9. The grand jury indicted the defendant for violating 18 U.S.C. § 2312. __CR__

10. Counsel attempted to offer the psychologist's testimony into evidence. __CR CI__

11. The plaintiff brought suit in the United States District Court for the Southern District of New York. _____C/_____

12. The jury awarded the plaintiff $500,000 in compensatory damages. _____C/_____

13. The parties refused to settle the case, so they had to litigate. _____

14. The defendant took a plea. _____

15. The judge charged the jury. _____

16. The witness took the stand. _____

17. The litigation began in the Supreme Court. _____

18. The plaintiff sought punitive damages. _____

WORD STUDY | *Bar, Esquire, Esq., Lawyer Up*

Bar can mean to prohibit, a legal association, or a licensing examination:

▸ *Prohibit*: The Gun Free School Zone Act *bars* (prohibits) a person from possessing certain weapons within 1,000 feet of a school.

▸ *Legal association*: A *bar* can also refer to an entity composed of people who are admitted to practice as lawyers in a state. A state or local *bar* association is a group of people who meet and provide many services to the public and to lawyers.

▸ *Licensing examination*: A *bar examination* is the test given in a state to become a lawyer, which, if passed, qualifies the individual to apply to that state's authority for the privilege to practice law.

Esquire, abbreviated *Esq.*, is often used to refer to an attorney admitted to the bar.

To *lawyer up* means to hire a lawyer to protect oneself. For example: "The defendant *lawyered up*, so the police had to stop questioning her."

EXERCISE 31 | Selected "People" in a Court Case

Instructions: Match the terms in the left-hand column with the definitions in the right-hand column by writing the letter of the definition in front of the number of the term. The first one is completed as a model.

Terms

_p_ **1.** Party or litigant

_____ **2.** Plaintiff

_____ **3.** Defendant

_____ **4.** Attorney for the plaintiff

_____ **5.** Attorney for the defendant

_____ **6.** District attorney

_____ **7.** United States attorney

_____ **8.** Solicitor general

_____ **9.** Judge

_____ **10.** Justice

_____ **11.** Administrative law judge

_____ **12.** Court reporter

_____ **13.** Appellant

_____ **14.** Appellee

_____ **15.** Petitioner

_____ **16.** Respondent

_____ **17.** Witness

_____ **18.** Jury (a juror)

_____ **19.** Esq.

Definitions

a. The person responding to a petition

b. The appealing party

c. The person filing a petition in a court

d. Judges of the United States Supreme Court

e. The person who gives evidence (testifies or takes the stand) at a trial

f. The person who presides over a trial

g. The person who transcribes or records court proceedings

h. The party who is not appealing

i. The local prosecutor in counties throughout a state

j. The lawyer who represents the party being sued

k. The lawyer who represents the party bringing the action

l. The group of people who discuss the evidence and return a verdict

m. Shorthand for a lawyer admitted to the bar

n. The judge presiding over an administrative proceeding

o. The party being sued (defending him- or herself)

p. A person or legal entity taking one side in a lawsuit

q. The attorney who represents the federal government in a given federal district

r. The attorney who represents the United States of America in cases before the United States Supreme Court

s. The party bringing (commencing) the litigation

Where Do Federal Trials Take Place?

Article III Courts

The following are Article III federal courts:

1. United States district courts, conducting trials in certain federal civil and criminal cases, when the court has the power (jurisdiction) to hear those cases.

   There are other Article III courts, separate and apart from the US district courts, which hear specific types of federal cases, as follows:

2. Bankruptcy courts, hearing bankruptcy proceedings in each judicial district. A person or entity may apply to court to be protected from debtors or to reorganize a corporation.
3. The US Court of International Trade, hearing customs cases. Customs are payments for bringing goods into the United States.
4. The US Court of Federal Claims, hearing claims against the United States.

Article I Courts

Courts established by Congress under its Article I powers are called *Article I courts* or *legislative courts* and are created "to carry out a legislative power [an enumerated power as specified in Article I, § 8], such as the determination of taxes or the governance of the armed forces."[4] But these courts do not have full Article III powers, such as the power to determine questions of constitutional law.[5] The judges in Article I courts are not appointed for life.

The following are Article I courts:

1. The US Tax Court, hearing taxpayer claims when the Internal Revenue Service determines that taxes are owed.
2. The US Court of Appeals for the Armed Forces, reviewing certain cases involving Armed Forces Court of Criminal Appeals.
3. The US Court of Appeals for Veterans Claims, reviewing decisions of the Board of Veterans' Appeals. Veterans are people who previously served in the one of the armed forces, such as the army, the navy, or the marines. A veteran may be colloquially called a *vet*, not to be confused with the verb *to vet*, meaning "to closely examine." *Vet* is also short for *veterinarian*, or a doctor for animals.

EXERCISE 32 | The Judiciary and Related Terminology

Instructions: Circle "True" or "False" after the following statements.

1. Article III judges preside in state courts.   **True   False**

2. The adversaries in a case are the plaintiff and the defendant who compete to win a case.   **True   False**

3. A trial court judge charges the jury, giving instructions such as the elements of a crime.   **True   False**

4. A litigant can mean either a plaintiff or a defendant.   **True   False**

5. A trial is a higher court review of a lower court decision.   **True   False**

6. In an appeals court, the judges hear witness testimony.   **True   False**

7. *To try* is a verb, related to the noun *trial*. An attorney tries a case in a trial court.   **True   False**

8. An *en banc* panel is a group of appellate judges who can rehear a case after the same level of appellate court hears the original appeal.   **True   False**

9. A United States district court is a federal court.   **True   False**

10. Three judges in total preside over a single case in a trial court.   **True   False**

11. A majority means more than half. A majority in the United States Supreme Court is a vote of four justices.   **True   False**

12. A jury may decide a case in the federal appeals court.   **True   False**

13. A bench trial is a trial in which there is no jury.   **True   False**

14. The judge charges the jury in both civil and criminal trials.   **True   False**

15. A plaintiff in a trial court proceeding can be the appellee in an appellate court proceeding.   **True   False**

16. A defendant in the trial court can be the appellant in an appellate court proceeding.   **True   False**

17. When a party files a petition for a writ of injunction or a writ of habeas corpus, the parties are called *petitioner* and *defendant*.   **True   False**

18. A party in a lawsuit may also be called a *prosecutor*.   **True   False**

Where Do Appeals Take Place in Federal Courts?

Federal Appeals Courts (United States Courts of Appeals)

If the losing party chooses to appeal, a federal appeals court reviews the decision of the US district court. A criminal defendant who is found guilty at trial can appeal the guilty verdict, but if a criminal defendant is found *not guilty* after a trial, the prosecution cannot appeal.[6]

There are thirteen separate circuits throughout the entire United States. Therefore, with fifty separate states, more than one state combines with others to form a *circuit*. Circuits generally have the power to review cases that are appealed from any of the district courts within the states covered by those circuits.

The Thirteen Federal Appeals Courts and Sister Circuits

There are eleven numbered circuits, plus the United States Court of Appeals for the DC Circuit and the United States Court of Appeals for the Federal Circuit, hearing appeals from the ninety-four district courts. The different circuits are on the same level and are called *sister circuits* because they are related to each other, like sisters in the same level in a family tree. Here is a list of the thirteen federal circuits consisting of eleven numbered circuits and two named circuits:

1. First Circuit.
2. Second Circuit.
3. Third Circuit.
4. Fourth Circuit.
5. Fifth Circuit.
6. Sixth Circuit.
7. Seventh Circuit.
8. Eighth Circuit.
9. Ninth Circuit.
10. Tenth Circuit.
11. Eleventh Circuit.
12. The United States Court of Appeals for the District of Columbia Circuit hears appeals from the US District Court for the District of Columbia. Located on Constitution Avenue in the nation's capital, Washington, DC, this court hears many important cases, involving federal laws and regulations.
13. The Court of Appeals for the Federal Circuit, located in Washington, DC, hears appeals of specific types of cases such as patent law decisions from any of the ninety-four federal district courts and appeals from the Court of International Trade and the Federal Court of Claims.

The following map shows both the federal districts (the district names are written in on the map, within one particular state) and the eleven numbered federal circuits (the numbers in the black circles). This illustrates which federal appellate courts can hear appeals from the various federal trial courts throughout the United States, referred to as the *path of appeal*.

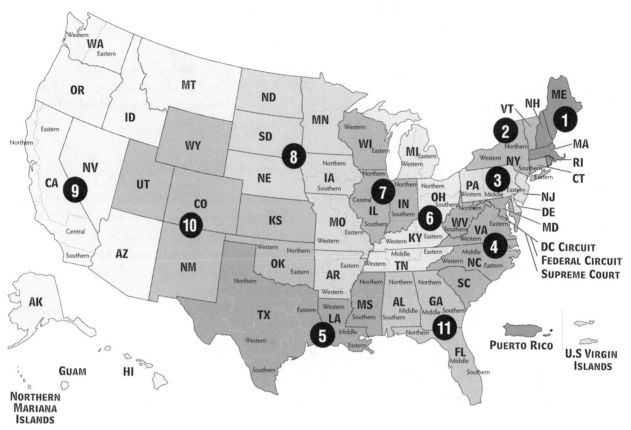

Federal trial courts and federal circuit courts.

Each state has at least one federal district, and some states have more than one federal geographic district. For example, look at the larger states toward the center of the United States, including Wyoming (WY), Colorado (CO), Kansas (KS), and New Mexico (NM). The map includes only the state name; each of these states has only one judicial district as follows:

▸ The United States (federal) District Court for the District of Wyoming
▸ The United States (federal) District Court for the District of Colorado
▸ The United States (federal) District Court for the District of Kansas
▸ The United States (federal) District Court for the District of New Mexico

Now look at the map for the state of Oklahoma (OK). There are three districts: the Western, Northern, and Eastern Districts.

Next, look at the map for the state of New York (NY) on the East Coast, all the way on the right side of the map. On the map, within New York State, you will see four words written: Southern, Eastern, Northern, and Western. That is because there are four separate federal districts in New York:

1. Southern District of New York (S.D.N.Y.), hearing both civil and criminal cases originating in New York, Bronx, Westchester, Rockland, Putnam, Orange, Dutchess, and Sullivan Counties
2. Eastern District of New York (E.D.N.Y.), hearing both civil and criminal cases originating in Brooklyn (Kings County), Queens, Richmond, Nassau, and Suffolk Counties
3. Northern District of New York (N.D.N.Y.), hearing both civil and criminal cases originating in upstate counties including Albany, Broome, Cayuga, and others.
4. Western District of New York (W.D.N.Y.), hearing both civil and criminal cases in upstate counties including Allegany, Erie, Genesee, and others.

Federal trial courts hear both civil and criminal cases. The place of trial may depend on where the case arose or where the crime took place, as Congress prescribes. A person who allegedly robbed a federal bank that is located in Manhattan could be tried (the trial would take place) in the United States District Court for the Southern District of New York. A person who allegedly brought illegal drugs into the United States through Kennedy Airport could be tried in the United States District Court for the Eastern District of New York because Kennedy Airport is located in Queens County. Attorneys make important decisions on where to file suit in civil cases on the basis of specific rules.

EXERCISE 33	Federal District Courts

Instructions: Look at the map on the previous page and write the names of the district courts for each of the following states:

1. Rhode Island (RI):

2. California (CA):

3. Texas (TX):

4. Florida (FL):

5. Idaho (ID):

6. Washington State (WA):

7. North Dakota (ND):

Appeals from Federal District Courts to Circuit Courts

The round numbers on the map (page 116) represent the circuit number that hears appeals from district courts within a group of states. For example, an appeal from any of the district courts in Utah (UT), Colorado (CO), Wyoming (WY), Kansas (KS), Oklahoma (OK), and New Mexico (NM) would be brought to the Tenth Circuit Court of Appeals.

Appeals from Federal Appeals Courts to the United States Supreme Court

The last federal court to which a party may appeal is the Supreme Court of the United States. The United States Supreme Court is located in Washington, DC, and consists of nine justices: one chief justice and eight associate justices, all nominated by the current president when a vacancy occurs, and confirmed by the Senate.

The Path of Appeal in Federal Courts

3. Final level of appeal: The United States Supreme Court
Certiorari: discretionary appeal from all 13 circuits

↑

2. First level of appeal to the Federal Appeals Courts (13 circuits): United States Courts of Appeals for the . . .

First Circuit (1st Cir.)	Second Circuit (2d Cir.)	Third Circuit (3d Cir.)	Fourth Circuit (4th Cir.)	Fifth Circuit (5th Cir.)	Sixth Circuit (6th Cir.)	Seventh Circuit (7th Cir.)	Eighth Circuit (8th Cir.)	Ninth Circuit (9th Cir.)	Tenth Circuit (10th Cir.)	Eleventh Circuit (11th Cir.)	D.C. Circuit (D.C. Cir.)	Federal Circuit (also hears patent and other cases)

↑ ↑ ↑ ↑ ↑ ↑ ↑ ↑ ↑ ↑ ↑ ↑ ↑

Mandatory appeals ("as of right") from the US district courts to the US courts of appeals listed directly above

1. Trials: Federal Trial Courts: United States District Courts in the State (or Territory) of . . .

Massa-chusetts Puerto Rico Maine New Hamp-shire Rhode Island	New York Connecti-cut Vermont	Delaware New Jersey Pennsyl-vania Virgin Islands	Virginia North Carolina South Carolina	Texas Louisiana Missis-sippi	Ohio Kentucky Tennessee Michigan	Wiscon-sin Illinois Indiana	North Dakota South Dakota Nebraska Minne-sota Iowa Missouri Arkansas	California Oregon Wash-ington (state) Idaho Montana Nevada Arizona Alaska Hawaii Guam Northern Marianas	Oklahoma Kansas Colorado New Mexico Utah Wyoming	Alabama Georgia Florida	D.C. (Wash-ington, DC)	Court of Inter-national Trade; US Court of Federal Claims

EXERCISE 34 | Appeals to the Circuit Courts

Instructions: Review "The Path of Appeal in Federal Courts" on the previous page, and then write which court hears an appeal from each of the following courts:

1. The United States District Court for the Northern District of Texas:

2. The United States District Court for the Central District of California:

3. The United States District Court for the Western District of Oklahoma:

4. The United States District Court for the Northern District of New York:

5. The United States District Court for the Eastern District of California:

6. The United States District Court for the District of Rhode Island:

7. The Second Circuit Court of Appeals:

8. The Eighth Circuit Court of Appeals:

9. The Court of Appeals for the Federal Circuit:

10. The United States Supreme Court:

11. The District of Columbia Circuit Court:

WORD STUDY | *Hon., Chief, Justice, Judge*

Hon. is an abbreviation for *Honorable*, here referring to judges. When addressing a judge, one would respectfully say, "Your Honor."

A *chief* is the person in the highest position, such as the leader of a business, agency, or other organization. The *chief justice* is the lead justice of the United States Supreme Court, whose correct title is the Chief Justice of the United States. The chief justice heads an important organization called the Federal Judicial Conference. This group consists of many federal judges who meet, discuss, and advise on issues concerning the day-to-day functions of the federal courts.

Depending on the court, the official title of a judge may be either *judge* or *justice*. In this context, both terms mean the person who presides over cases in a trial or appeals court.

- United States Supreme Court: The official title is *justice*. The lead justice is the *chief justice*. An attorney addressing a Supreme Court judge would use the term *justice*, such as "Justice Kagan" or "Justice Breyer."
- Federal district (trial) court judges and federal court of appeals judges: The official title is *judge*. The lead judge is the *chief judge*.

States may use different terminology. Consult each court's website to determine the official titles.

In printed court opinions, *J.* is an abbreviation for either *Judge* or *Justice*, depending on the court, and *J.J.* is the plural, meaning two or more judges or justices. *C.J.* means *Chief Judge* or *Chief Justice*, depending on the court.

Justice can also be a noun, which does not mean a person but, in essence, means fairness. Courts should do *justice*, or be fair.

Judicial Nomination and Qualifications of Federal Judges

Under Article II, § 2, of the Federal Constitution, the president of the United States nominates US Supreme Court justices and other federal judges with the "advice and consent of the Senate." The Senate holds a hearing to *vet* the candidate's qualifications before appointment. The Constitution does not list any specific qualifications required for Supreme Court justices, though an unqualified nonlawyer would not be nominated by the president or confirmed (approved) by the Senate.

US Supreme Court justices have varied backgrounds. One famous former justice, Oliver Wendell Holmes, served on the highest court in the state of Massachusetts, called the Massachusetts Supreme Court. Another famous former justice, Benjamin N. Cardozo, served on the highest court in the state of New York, called the

John Jay was the first chief justice of the United States, serving 1789–95.

New York Court of Appeals. Justice Elena Kagan, a current justice, was never a judge but was previously a dean of Harvard Law School and the United States solicitor general (the lawyer who represents the United States government in cases before the United States Supreme Court).

The president of the United States nominates federal judges, the chief justice, and the attorney general (the head of the Justice Department), as the Federal Constitution prescribes. One former president of the United States, William Howard Taft, served both as president (1909–13) and then as chief justice of the United States (1921–30).[7]

WORD STUDY | *SCOTUS, High Court, Top Court, Court of Last Resort*

An acronym is a series of letters, pronounced together as a single word, that is formed from certain letters in separate, related words:

▸ *SCOTUS* (pronounced as one word: "Skotus") is an acronym for the *Supreme Court of the United States.*

▸ *SOX* (pronounced as one word: "Soks") is an acronym for the *Sarbanes–Oxley Act,* codified in the U.S.C.

▸ *POTUS* refers to the *President of the United States,* and *FLOTUS* refers to the *First Lady of the United States,* the president's wife.

The US Supreme Court is sometimes referred to as the *high court* or the *top court* because of its place at the highest point, or top, of the courts, as shown in the following pyramid. There is no other court higher in level than the Supreme Court of the United States, and a party losing in the United States Supreme Court cannot have the case reviewed again. The highest court in each state may also be referred to as the *high court* or the *top court,* such as *California's high court* or *New York's top court,* as illustrated in the following figures:

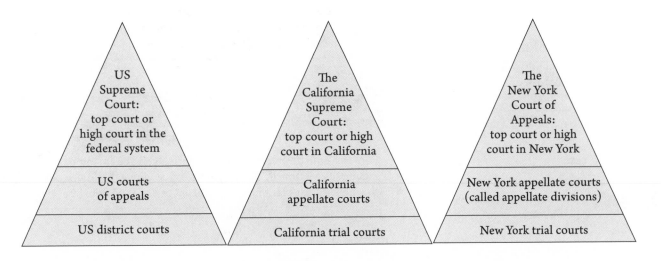

A *last resort* describes a situation in which a person has a problem, has tried many options, and the last option or *last resort* is the one final effort to solve that problem. If a person lost his keys in a school building and looked everywhere, such as his coat pockets, under desks, in other classrooms, and in the hallway, he might state that his *last resort* is to contact the guard who sits at the front door to find out if anyone turned in the keys: the guard is his *last resort*, or the last place he could look to find the keys.

A *court of last resort* is the last court in either the federal or state system in which a party can seek review. There is no court higher than a *court of last resort*.

- SCOTUS is the federal court of last resort, the last court that may hear issues of federal law.
- A state's highest court is the state court of last resort on issues of state law. (But a party may appeal to the United States Supreme Court from the state's highest court on issues of federal law.)

These are the last courts in which a person will have an opportunity to seek the court's assistance to review the case.

WORD STUDY | *Appeal, Mandatory Review, Discretionary Review, Certiorari, Certification*

United States Supreme Court	**Discretionary Review** Appeal to the US Supreme Court The US Supreme Court chooses whether to grant certiorari and hear a case or to deny certiorari and refuse to hear the case.
Federal appeals courts (US courts of appeals)	**Mandatory Review** Appeal to the federal appeals court The court must hear certain appeals, if the losing party chooses to appeal. The higher court reviews the lower court decision for claimed errors raised in the trial court below.
Federal trial courts (US district courts)	

Appeal: A party who loses at the trial level or the appellate level may appeal to a higher court.[8]

Mandatory review, appeal as of right: *Mandatory* comes from the verb *to mandate*, or require. When a higher court must review (hear an appeal) from a lower court, it is called *mandatory* or *required review*. US courts of appeals must hear certain appeals from US district courts: the review is mandatory, and the losing party in the trial court has an automatic right to appeal certain decisions, called an *appeal as of right*.[9]

Discretionary review: *Discretion* means "choice." When a higher court has discretion to review cases from a lower court, it chooses which cases to hear. The US Supreme Court generally has discretion to choose which cases it hears. The appealing party must first file what is called a *petition for a writ of certiorari* to the US Supreme Court requesting that the court exercise its discretion and choose to hear the case. In these requests, the appealing party is filing a petition and is now called a *petitioner*. The losing party in the federal appeals court or state high court, responding to the petition, is called a *respondent*.

Certiorari: A losing party may request that the US Supreme Court exercise its discretion and hear an appeal from either a federal appeals court or the highest court of a state on a federal issue. This request is made in a *petition for a writ of certiorari*. In this petition and supporting briefs, a party explains to the court why it should hear the case.

The abbreviation for *certiorari* is *cert*. If cert is granted, it means only that at least four of the nine US Supreme Court justices have agreed to hear the case. And when the US Supreme Court grants cert, it is, in effect, ordering the lower court to send the record in the case to the US Supreme Court. The United States Supreme Court grants certiorari and hears approximately eighty out of 7,000–8,000 petitions it receives each year.[10]

If the Supreme Court justices grant cert, the parties then file written arguments summarizing their positions, in what are called *merits briefs*. There is ordinarily an oral argument by the attorneys before the justices.

If cert is denied, it means that the US Supreme Court has refused to hear the case. That is the end of the case, and no further appeal is possible.

Certification: Certification is a process under which a federal court asks a state high court a question. In certain situations, federal courts can certify or ask a question to a state's high court as to how it would interpret state law in the case.

EXERCISE 35 | # Which Federal Court?

Instructions: Write the level of federal court in which each of the following actions took place: a federal trial court, a federal appeals court, or the US Supreme Court.

1. The top court granted cert:

2. The high court decided that the Affordable Care Act is a constitutional exercise of Congress's taxing power:

3. The circuit court judges denied the petition for en banc review:

4. The jury decided that the defendant was not guilty:

5. The Second Circuit Court of Appeals heard the appeal:

6. The trial took place in the US District Court for the Eastern District of Pennsylvania:

7. The justices exercised discretionary review and granted cert:

8. SCOTUS denied cert:

9. The three-judge panel had mandatory review of the federal trial court's judgment:

10. The federal court of last resort declined to hear the appeal:

WORD STUDY | ## *On the Merits, To Have Merit*

The expression *on the merits* arises when describing certain court decisions in a case. A *decision on the merits* describes a decision on the underlying case on the ground that the party brought suit. By contrast, when there is a decision that does not resolve the underlying case, it is a decision that is *not on the merits*.

Decisions that are on the merits:

- In a contract case, whether there was a breach (violation of) the contract terms
- In a negligence case, whether the defendant acted negligently

Decisions that *are not* on the merits:

- *The Supreme Court deciding to grant or deny certiorari.* The court decides if it will hear the case: it is not a decision on the merits or value of the party's claim in a case.

▶ *Standing.* A court may decide if a person has a sufficient "personal stake in the outcome" with an injury that the court can remedy.[11]

▶ *Selected pretrial motions.* Subject matter jurisdiction: whether the court has the power to hear the case; or statute of limitations: whether the time limit for bringing suit has passed.

Merits cases are cases in which the court will address the underlying issues.

By contrast, the expression *to have merit* refers to the value of or success of a legal or factual issue. A judge deciding if an argument, claim, appeal, or pretrial motion *has merit* is deciding whether it is one that has some value, or has a potentially successful basis in law, as in the following example:

> There is no merit to the assertion that compliance with [the statute] should be excused.[12]

Why Does the United States Supreme Court Grant Certiorari?

The Supreme Court does not always explain why it decides to hear or refuses to hear a case. However, sometimes, in the beginning of a written opinion, the US Supreme Court will state why it granted certiorari and heard the case. When the court explains why it granted cert, the court is being transparent (open and not secret) by telling the public why it agreed to hear the case.

EXERCISE 36 | ## US Supreme Court Review

Instructions: Read the United States Supreme Court rule, and then answer the following questions.

Rule 10. Considerations Governing Review on Certiorari

Review on a writ of certiorari is not a matter of right, but of judicial discretion. A petition for a writ of certiorari will be granted only for compelling reasons. The following, although neither controlling nor fully measuring the Court's discretion, indicate the character of the reasons the Court considers: (a) a United States court of appeals has entered a decision in conflict with the decision of another United States court of appeals on the same important matter; has decided an important federal question in a way that conflicts with a decision by a state court of last resort; or has so far departed from the accepted and usual course of judicial proceedings, or sanctioned such a departure by a lower court, as to call for an exercise of this Court's supervisory power; (b) a state court of last resort has decided an important federal question in a way that conflicts with the decision of another state court of last resort or of a United States court of appeals; (c) a state court or a United States court of appeals has decided an important question of federal law that has not been, but should be, settled by this Court, or has decided an important federal question in a way that conflicts with relevant decisions of this Court. A petition for a writ of certiorari is rarely granted when the asserted error consists of erroneous factual findings or the misapplication of a properly stated rule of law.[13]

1. Is the US Supreme Court review mandatory or discretionary? What does this mean?

2. In Rule 10(a), does the "United States court of appeals" refer to federal or state courts? What is another name for these courts?

3. In Rule 10(b), which courts are the "state court[s] of last resort"?

4. In Rule 10(c), which specific courts are mentioned?

WORD STUDY | *Phrasal and Other Verbs in the Context of Court Decisions*

Read the following headlines, which explain a court's action, and observe if each scenario describes a decision *on the merits*.

1. *To back* means to support or authorize.

   Court *Backs* Hot-Button Obama Power Plant Rule[14]

   A federal court backed, or supported and authorized, a federal agency's decision to promulgate a rule (during the Obama administration) and thus found that the rule could remain in effect. The Environmental Protection Agency rule concerns the hot-button issue of climate change, and the rule's validity was challenged in court. This is a decision on the merits.

2. *To OK* means to authorize or allow.

   Del. Justices *OK* Toss of $13M Viacom-Redstone Pay Suit[15]

   Justices in Delaware's Supreme Court agreed with a lower court's decision to *toss* (throw out or dismiss) a lawsuit and allowed the lower court decision to stand. The headline itself does not inform the reader why the case was dismissed, whether it was or was not on the merits.

3. *To take* means to grant certiorari.

   Justices *Take* Case on President's Power to Detain[16]

The United States Supreme Court agreed to hear the case but at the time of the headline had not yet issued a decision on the merits, only on granting cert.

4. *To tackle* has a connotation of addressing a challenge. In the infinitive, *to tackle* frequently combines with *issue*, such as "the court will tackle an issue of first impression" (i.e., the first time the court is deciding an issue).

    Supreme Court to *Tackle* Copyright Registrations Circuit Split[17]

    The US Supreme Court decided to tackle and agreed to resolve a challenging copyright law case. The "circuit split" means that some lower federal appeals courts reached a different decision on this issue than other federal appeals courts. At the time of the headline, this was not yet a decision on the merits. The infinitive form "to tackle" indicates that there is an action that the court will take in the future.

5. *To rule* means to issue a ruling, or a judicial determination, on a "point of law or on the case as a whole."[18]

    Justices *Rule* for Police in Deadly Car Chase[19]

    The US Supreme Court determined that the police were justified in using force in a high-speed car chase during which the police shot and killed a driver and passenger. This is a decision on the merits.

    The following headlines use phrasal verbs, which are verbs that change meaning, depending on the preposition or adverb that follows the verb. Some commonplace phrasal verbs that could be used in daily speech are listed in appendix 2

6. *To take on* means to take responsibility for something, often to *take on* or address a challenge. In the context of a court's decision, *take on* can mean deciding a challenging case.

    Supreme Court *Takes On* Major Fourth Amendment Case[20]

    The US Supreme Court decided to address a challenging case concerning the government's right to obtain data from an individual's cell phone. Courts have had to decide how to balance a person's right to be free from "unreasonable searches and seizures" under the US Constitution's Fourth Amendment with the need for law enforcement to obtain evidence to prove that a crime was committed. This was not yet a decision on the merits, only on the decision to grant cert, indicated by the court's decision to "take on" and resolve this important case.

7. *To stand by* means to support a decision. A parent who supports a child's job choice *stands by* or supports the child's decision. When a higher court *stands by* a decision, the court affirms (agrees with) the lower court decision or decides not to overrule (change) a previous principle of law that the court established in a previous case.

    In Spider-Man Toy Patent Case, Supreme Court *Stands by* Past Decision[21]

The US Supreme Court stood by its previous decision, deciding to leave a rule intact and not to overrule or change the rule originally decided in an earlier case. The court also affirmed the lower federal appeals court decision. This is a decision on the merits.

8. *To let stand* means to leave something in place. If the court *lets stand* a lower court decision, the decision of the lower court remains (stands) as it was, and the court does not change the lower court decision. This commonly occurs when a higher court with discretionary appeal powers refused to hear the case, leaving the lower court decision intact.

Supreme Court *Lets Stand* Ruling Favoring Ride-Hailing Services[22]

The US Supreme Court left the federal appeals court decision intact (unchanged) and refused to grant cert. This is not a decision on the merits in the US Supreme Court.

9. *To turn away* means to not allow someone or something to enter a place. If a movie theater has all of the seats occupied, the theater will *turn away* additional customers who want to see that movie. *Turn away* is used when a person or an entity, such as a country, rejects or does not allow people to enter. A country that *turns away* refugees seeking asylum rejects or forbids the refugees from entering the country. When the Supreme Court *turns away* a case, it means that the court refused to hear the case, denying certiorari.

Supreme Court *Turns Away* Challenge to Connecticut's Semiautomatic Weapon Ban[23]

The court turned the case away, refusing to grant cert. This is not a decision on the merits in the US Supreme Court because the court simply refused to hear the case.

10. *To side with* means to decide in a person's or other entity's favor. In a court case, there are two sides, or at least two parties on either side of a case: one side is the plaintiff, and the other side is the defendant. When a jury *sides with* a defendant, the jury has decided that the defendant wins; when a jury *sides with* a plaintiff, the jury has decided that the plaintiff wins. When a court (one or more judges deciding a case) *sides with* a party, the court has decided which party wins.

Justices *Side with* Colorado Baker on Same-Sex Wedding Cake[24]

The US Supreme Court sided with, or agreed with, one side (one party in the case), the baker. This was a decision on the merits.

WORD STUDY | *Transparent (adjective), Transparency (noun); Opaque (adjective), Opacity (noun)*

Transparent can mean open or see-through. The opposite of *transparent* is *opaque*, which means closed or not see-through. If we look at the window of a building or a car and can see inside, the window is transparent, or see-through. The contents inside the building or car are visible to the person looking through the window.

An open window that a person can see through is transparent.

A painted or blocked window that a person cannot see through is opaque.

Government actors are *transparent* when they act openly, making records available to the public, explaining their actions, and allowing people to attend meetings, hearings, and trials. Government actors are *opaque* when they do not allow public access to documents, meetings, hearings, and trials and do not inform the public about their actions.

There are many terms that have some aspect of opacity (secrecy) or transparency (openness).

Secrecy or Opacity

Anonymous, anonymity: *Anonymous* is an adjective that means unnamed, without identification. An *anonymous* tip is information from a person who has not given a name. An *anonymous* survey asks people to answers questions without putting their names on the survey. *Anonymity* is a noun. A person who does not want to be named or identified would request *anonymity* as in this example: "The witness called the police but requested *anonymity*. She feared for her safety and did want the person who committed the crime to know her name or identity."*

Gag order: A gag is literally a piece of cloth that goes into someone's mouth and prevents the person from talking. A gag order is not an actual piece of cloth but is a symbol for a judge's order (command) that prohibits someone from disclosing information. For example, during a trial, a judge may issue a *gag order* prohibiting the lawyers and parties from speaking with the press and the public and from discussing

* *Roe* and *Doe* (Jane Roe or John Doe) are called *pseudonyms* (fake names), used to preserve a person's anonymity or when the person's real name is not known. In *Roe v. Wade*, 410 U.S. 113 (1973), the plaintiff used the pseudonym *Roe*.

what took place in the courtroom. Since this is an order from a judge, a party who disobeys this order could be subject to contempt proceedings.

Veil: A *veil* is a cover. A *corporate veil* is a symbol for protecting officials of a corporation from personal responsibility in a business. When a court *pierces the corporate veil*, it means that the officials are not protected, in effect no longer covered by a veil, and may be personally responsible for the business's actions. To *lift a veil* means to uncover or make something transparent. To *unveil* can mean to announce: "The company *unveiled* plans to expand into new areas."

Privilege against self-incrimination; take the fifth: The Fifth Amendment to the United States Constitution states that a person "shall not be compelled in any criminal case to be a witness against himself." This is called the *privilege against self-incrimination*. When a person may be subject to criminal consequences due to questioning, the Federal Constitution can protect that person. In criminal cases, defendants do not have to testify against themselves at trial. A person who is subpoenaed (officially called) to give testimony at a congressional hearing or a civil or criminal trial may *take the fifth*,* or invoke the person's Fifth Amendment right not to give testimony against oneself. That person does not have to answer questions, which would be incriminating (would subject that person to criminal consequences). However, if a person *taking the fifth* is given immunity, or protection from criminal consequences for giving testimony, he or she must give testimony.

* *Take the fifth* has become a colloquial expression used in nonlegal contexts, when a person does not want to answer a question, sometimes to convey humor: "Did you eat the last piece of cake?" "I take the fifth!"

Undercover or *under cover*: A person who operates *under cover* does so in secrecy. *Plainclothes cops* are police officers who wear regular clothes and not their police uniforms while investigating a crime in order to operate *under cover* and hide their identity. As one example, *undercover* officers may work in police operations called a *buy and bust* in which they buy illegal drugs and then bust, or arrest, the seller. Anyone who intentionally hides his or her identity may be considered as acting *undercover*, such as store guards who are not in uniform to catch people who steal from the store.

Seal: A *seal* is a symbol for something that is closed. This term frequently arises with respect to court records, when a judge *seals* records to prohibit them from being disclosed to the public. A young person who commits a first low-level crime may receive a favorable disposition from a judge, and the judge may then order that the records be *sealed*, or closed, so that no one can obtain those records.

Shield law: These laws shield or protect reporters from having to disclose their confidential sources under certain circumstances.

Hush money: *Hush* is a term that means "to be quiet," "to stop talking." A person might ask someone else (colloquially) to *hush*, or be quiet, in order to ask that person to stop talking about something. *Hush money* is money that is paid to a person to keep quiet about something, often when something is controversial or even sometimes illegal.

Transparency

Leak: *Leak* is a term for information that a person discloses without permission of the speaker or writer. In government private meetings, when an attendee anonymously gives the press or public information discussed privately in that meeting, the person has *leaked* that information or given it out without authorization.

FOIA: The Freedom of Information Act, 5 U.S.C. § 552, is a federal statute that promotes transparency or openness in federal government by allowing people to obtain federal government records that the government has not previously disclosed. Individual states have Freedom of Information laws (FOIL), which authorize people to obtain information from individual state governments.

EXERCISE 37 | # Transparent or Opaque

Instructions: Write whether each of the following is transparent or opaque.

1. A judge closing the courtroom because an undercover police officer is testifying:

2. The United States Supreme Court granting certiorari without explaining why it did so:

3. The United States Supreme Court granting certiorari and explaining why it did so:

4. Congress holding hearings in closed-door session, without allowing cameras or members of the public to attend the hearing:

5. The Freedom of Information Act, which allows members of the public to obtain certain government records:

6. A judge of the Foreign Intelligence Surveillance Court (FISC) issuing a warrant,* which allows the government to listen to a person's telephone conversations without the person's knowledge:

* A *warrant* is a legal document that permits certain types of searches (search warrant) or the arrest of an individual (arrest warrant), as two examples.

7. A plaintiff signing a nondisclosure agreement (NDA), agreeing not to disclose the amount of money that the defendant paid after settling the case:

EXERCISE 38 | Certiorari and Transparency

Instructions: Read each of the case excerpts, and then answer the following questions.

Case 1: *BMW of North America, Inc., v. Gore*, 517 U.S. 559, 568 (1996)

Justice Stevens delivered the opinion of the Court:

Because we believed that a review of this case would help to illuminate "the character of the standard that will identify unconstitutionally excessive awards" of punitive damages, see *Honda Motor Co. v. Oberg*, 512 U. S. 415, 420 (1994), we granted certiorari.

1. Who delivered (presented) this opinion?

2. Was the United States Supreme Court transparent about the reason for granting cert?

3. What issue did the Supreme Court tackle by taking this case?

Case 2: *McBoyle v. United States*, 283 U.S. 25, 25 (1931)

Justice Holmes delivered the opinion of the Court:

The petitioner was convicted of [violating 18 U.S.C. §408 by] transporting from Ottawa, Illinois, to Guymon, Oklahoma, an airplane that he knew to have been stolen, and was sentenced to serve three years' imprisonment and to pay a fine of $2,000. The judgment was affirmed by the Circuit Court of Appeals for the Tenth Circuit. A writ of certiorari was granted by this Court on the question whether the National Motor Vehicle Theft Act applies to aircraft. Reversed.

1. Who delivered (presented) this opinion?

2. Was this a federal or state crime? How do you know?

3. Was the US Supreme Court transparent about the reason for granting cert?

4. Did the US Supreme Court stand by the lower court decision in this case?

5. Did the US Supreme Court let the lower court decision stand?

Case 3: *Miranda v. Arizona*, 384 U.S. 436, 441–42 (1966)

Certiorari to the Supreme Court of Arizona. Chief Justice Warren delivered the opinion of the Court:

[Decided] with . . . *Vignera v. New York*, on certiorari to the Court of Appeals of New York and . . . *Westover v. United States*, on certiorari to the United States Court of Appeals for the Ninth Circuit . . . and . . . *California v. Stewart*, on certiorari to the Supreme Court of California.

We granted certiorari in these cases . . . in order further to explore some facets of the problems, thus exposed, of applying the [Fifth Amendment's] privilege against self-incrimination to in-custody interrogation, and to give concrete constitutional guidelines for law enforcement agencies and courts to follow.

1. Who delivered (presented) this opinion?

2. When the US Supreme Court granted cert, it consolidated (joined) cases involving a similar issue from different courts. Did these cases come from state or federal courts?

3. Was the US Supreme Court transparent about the reasons for granting cert?

4. Why did the US Supreme Court rule on this case?

Case 4: *North Carolina Department of Transportation v. Crest St. Community Council, Inc.*, 479 U.S. 6, 7, 11 (1986)

Justice O'Connor delivered the opinion of the Court:

This case presents the question whether a court may award attorney's fees under the Civil Rights Attorney's Fees Awards Act of 1976, 42 U.S.C. §1988, in a separate federal action not to enforce any of the civil rights laws listed in §1988, but solely to recover attorney's fees.

The Court of Appeals [for the Fourth Circuit] held that §1988 allowed a separate action for fees, although it acknowledged the contrary holdings of other courts. See *Horacek v. Thone*, 710 F.2d 496, 499 (CA8 1983); *Estes v. Tuscaloosa County*, 696 F.2d 898, 901 (CA11 1983); *Latino Project, Inc. v. City of Camden*, 701 F.2d 262 (CA3 1983). We granted certiorari, to resolve the Circuit conflict, 474 U.S. 1049 (1986), and now reverse.

1. Did this case originate in a state or a federal court?

2. Was the United States Supreme Court transparent about the reason for granting cert?

3. What does the citation "42 U.S.C. § 1988" inform the reader?

4. The "CA" in parentheses is short for *court of appeals*, and the number gives the federal circuit number. Which courts' precedents does the court cite, and why does the court cite these precedents?

5. Why did the Supreme Court take this case?

Case 5: *Dickerson v. United States*, 530 U.S. 428 (2000)

C.J. Rehnquist delivered the opinion of the Court:
    Because of the importance of the questions raised by the Court of Appeals' decision, we granted certiorari, 528 U. S. 1045 (1999), and now reverse.

1. *C.J.* is an abbreviation for *Chief Justice*. Who delivered this opinion?

2. Was the United States Supreme Court transparent about the reason for granting cert?

3. Why did the Supreme Court take on this issue?

Case 6: *Hollingsworth v. Angelone*, 537 U.S. 875, 875 (2002)

The petition for a writ of certiorari is denied.

1. Did the United States Supreme Court issue a decision on the merits?

2. Was the United States Supreme Court transparent about its cert decision?

3. Did the US Supreme Court rule on the issue in this case?

WORD STUDY | *Settled Law*

The term *settle* in a legal context may refer to parties agreeing to end a civil suit. *Settled law* has a different meaning: law that is well established, consistently followed, sometimes clearing up inconsistencies in previous decisions is *settled law*.

United States Supreme Court Rule 10 states that the court can grant certiorari when "a state court or a United States court of appeals has decided an important question of federal law that has not been, but should be, *settled* by this Court" (emphasis added). *Settled* here means clearly and finally decided, clearing up inconsistencies in decisions of other lower courts. When the law is not clear and different lower courts have issued inconsistent interpretations of the same question of law,[25] such as the meaning of a statutory term, the law is *unsettled*.

Courts of last resort clarify the law to make it consistent, so that lower courts apply the same rule. The US Supreme Court therefore might grant certiorari to *settle*, or clearly decide, an important question, which a state and federal court have decided inconsistently. State courts of last resort may choose to hear cases to *settle* the law of that state, that is, to clarify inconsistent rulings between lower state courts. However, even when a court *settles the law*, that law could later be changed or overruled if the court or other governmental entity later decides that the law should change.

A custodial interrogation

In *Miranda v. Arizona*, 384 U.S. 436 (1966), the United States Supreme Court established a rule regarding when law enforcement officers may interrogate (question) a person who is in custody: "Prior to any questioning, the person must be warned that he has a right to remain silent, that any statement he does make may be used as evidence against him, and that he has a right to the presence of an attorney, either retained or appointed." *Miranda v. Arizona*, 384 U.S. 436, 444–45.

Miranda is *settled law*. Before interrogating a person who is in custody, law enforcement officers must give these warnings, set forth in *Miranda*.

When a person in custody answers a police officer's questions and, as one example, confesses (admits) to committing a crime, later, during the court case, the prosecution would seek to have a jury (or the judge during a bench trial) hear this confession, that is, admit the confession into evidence.

Miranda is settled law, and a judge must find, before allowing the confession into evidence, that the person received the *Miranda* warnings and, if so, that the confession was made voluntarily. Without the jury present, the judge would hear the police officer's testimony about the interrogation. If the judge finds, for example, that police did not give the *Miranda* warnings (and there was no exception excusing the lack of warnings) or the person did not understand English and did not understand the warnings, the judge would *suppress** the confession, and the prosecution cannot use this confession in the court case against the defendant.

* In a *suppression hearing*, a judge in a criminal case determines whether certain evidence is admissible at trial or whether it should be suppressed (kept out) at a trial.

The Powers of the Federal Judiciary

Federal, state, and local courts must have jurisdiction, or the power, to adjudicate cases, interpret laws, and issue binding decisions affecting the parties' rights. Recall that Article I, § 8, enumerates federal legislative powers; similarly, Article III, § 2, specifies federal judicial power to hear certain types of cases.

In federal courts, "jurisdiction is a question of whether a federal court has the power, under the Constitution or laws of the United States, to hear a case."[26] State and local courts must have jurisdiction to hear cases as well. Here are some general overviews of selected types of jurisdiction.

1. *Original jurisdiction.* In this context, *original jurisdiction* means where a case originates or begins. Federal trial (district) courts and state trial courts are courts of *original jurisdiction*, that is, the first court that hears a case and where a case begins. In certain situations, the United States Supreme Court has *original jurisdiction*. Here is one example of original jurisdiction, codified in 28 U.S.C. § 1251(a): "The Supreme Court shall have original and exclusive jurisdiction of all controversies between two or more States."

2. *Exclusive jurisdiction. Exclusive* means to exclude others or to be limited to one person or entity. For example, a parent with exclusive custody of a child has the sole right to take care of the child, to the exclusion of the other parent. Federal courts have exclusive jurisdiction, or the sole right to hear certain types of cases, to the exclusion of state courts, as certain federal statutes provide. One such area is bankruptcy; there are specific federal bankruptcy courts that have the exclusive power to hear bankruptcy cases. This means that state courts cannot hear bankruptcy cases as specified by federal statute, 28 U.S.C. § 1334: Except as prescribed in the statute, "[t]he district courts shall have original and exclusive jurisdiction of all cases under title 11 [bankruptcy]."

3. *Supplemental jurisdiction, Concurrent jurisdiction. Supplemental* means "in addition to." *Concurrent* means "at the same time." Sometimes, courts may decide issues of federal and state law concurrently. Under certain circumstances, the federal trial court can hear all of these claims in one single case. In addition, if the federal courts do not have exclusive jurisdiction over the subject matter, a state court could hear

The Thurgood Marshall United States Courthouse, housing the United States Court of Appeals, 2d Circuit.

The Supreme Court of the State of New York, Trial Term, New York County

Two courts next to each other in lower Manhattan. Which is a state court and, which is a federal court? A lawyer must know in which court to initially commence a case. Which court has jurisdiction, or the power, to hear that case?

certain cases adjudicating federal, state, and local issues. It would be extraordinarily expensive and wasteful to have three different trials in three different levels of court:

> Concurrent jurisdiction in state and federal courts over claims arising from federal law is presumed. The Constitution does not mandate the creation of any federal courts other than the United States Supreme Court. Thus, the drafters of the Constitution originally contemplated that state courts would serve as trial courts for the adjudication of federal law, along with any federal courts that Congress might create.[27]

28 U.S.C. § 1367(a) provides for supplemental jurisdiction, subject to statutory exceptions: "In any civil action in which the district courts have original jurisdiction, the district courts shall have supplemental jurisdiction over all other claims that are so related to claims in the action within such original jurisdiction that they form part of the same case or controversy under Article III of the United States Constitution."

4. *Subject matter jurisdiction. Subject matter*, in this context, refers to the subjects or types of cases that courts have the power to decide as the Federal Constitution,

Article III, § 2, authorizes. State courts have subject matter jurisdiction over certain types of cases as well, and sometimes specific courts may hear cases according to certain monetary limits; local county courts in certain New York counties have subject matter jurisdiction over noncriminal cases in which a person seeks up to $25,000 and criminal cases in which a person has committed a crime within that specific local county.[28]

During a lawsuit, a defendant may claim that a court cannot hear the case because the court lacks the power to do so. In federal courts, a litigant may claim that the federal court lacks subject matter jurisdiction and that a state court should hear the case instead. The United States Constitution, Article III, § 2, addresses subject matter jurisdiction of federal courts:

> The Judicial Power shall extend to all Cases, in Law and Equity, arising under this Constitution, the Laws of the United States, and Treaties made, or which shall be made, under their Authority;—to all Cases affecting Ambassadors, other public Ministers and Consuls;—to all Cases of admiralty and maritime Jurisdiction;—to Controversies to which the United States shall be a Party;—to Controversies between two or more States . . . ; [and]—between Citizens of different States.

The following are selected Article III, § 2, provisions and corresponding federal statutes that further define federal court subject matter jurisdiction.

Federal question jurisdiction includes "[c]ases . . . arising under [a] this Constitution [the US Constitution's main articles and amendments (including the Bill of Rights)], [b] the Laws of the United States [federal laws in the U.S.C.], [c] Treaties* of the United States."	Corresponding federal statute: 28 U.S.C. § 1331
Admiralty and maritime jurisdiction: matters of the sea such as shipping and navigation.	Corresponding federal statute: 28 U.S.C. § 1333(1)
United States is a party: the United States sues another party, or a party sues the United States government.	Two corresponding federal statutes: 28 U.S.C. § 1345 and 28 U.S.C. § 1346
Diversity jurisdiction: "Controversies . . . between Citizens of different States." Diversity jurisdiction allows federal courts to adjudicate issues of state law when the citizens and others live in different states and the amount in controversy (relief requested in the form of money damages) exceeds $75,000.	Corresponding federal statute: 28 U.S.C. § 1332(a): "The district courts shall have original jurisdiction of all civil actions where the matter in controversy exceeds the sum or value of $75,000, exclusive of interest and costs, and is between—(1) citizens of different States; (2) citizens of a State and citizens or subjects of a foreign state."

* Recall from lesson 3.3 the difference between *treaties* and *treatises*.

EXERCISE 39 | # Criminal Cases

Instructions: Read the quotation from 18 U.S.C. § 3231, and then answer the following questions.

> The district courts of the United States shall have original jurisdiction, exclusive of the courts of the States, of all offenses against the laws of the United States.

1. What does "18 U.S.C." inform the reader?

2. Does the "district courts of the United States" mean federal trial courts, federal appeals courts, state trial courts, or state appeals court?

3. What does "original jurisdiction" mean in this context?

4. What does "exclusive of the courts of the States" mean?

5. Do "offenses against the laws of the United States" mean federal, state, or local laws?

LESSON 4.4 The Federal Judiciary's Source of Law

The following chart illustrates the sources from the three branches of government. Notice on the right that the common law comes from "judicial decisions."[29]

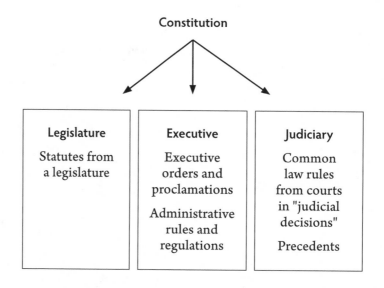

Constitution

Legislature	Executive	Judiciary
Statutes from a legislature	Executive orders and proclamations Administrative rules and regulations	Common law rules from courts in "judicial decisions" Precedents

Common law, common law rules, and *precedents* will later be discussed in more detail. For now, this lesson will focus on terminology that may arise in both federal and state court *cases* (i.e., during a civil lawsuit or a criminal prosecution).

WORD STUDY | *Case, Decision, Opinion; Citations; Reporters*

Case, Decision, Opinion
The written decision of a judge explaining a ruling before, during, or after a trial may be referred to as a *case,* a *decision,* or an *opinion,* as in the following examples:

- The judge issued a written opinion.
- The judge wrote a decision, explaining the ruling at trial.
- The case is printed in the *United States Reports*.

Case, *decision*, and *opinion* may mean the written ruling of a judge pretrial, during trial, or posttrial:

- Pretrial, a judge may write a decision, as two examples, to explain why the judge will not allow certain evidence to be introduced at a trial or to explain a decision on a pretrial motion, such as expiration of a time limit (statute of limitations) for commencing a case.
- During trial, a judge may write a decision, as one example, to explain why he or she refused to allow an expert witness to testify.
- Posttrial, a judge may write an opinion, as one example, explaining why he or she granted or denied a motion for a new trial on the basis of newly discovered evidence.

There are numerous possibilities.

Citations

A *citation* is a source's specific address or location, leading a reader to that source in a hard copy of a book or online. While most researchers may be familiar with citations of many sources such as books, articles, and internet sites, they may not be as familiar with case citations. Case citations contain a series of numbers and abbreviations such as this, as one example: *McBoyle v. United States*, 283 U.S. 25 (1931). The following chart explains each portion of this *McBoyle* citation:

Case name, abbreviated, underlined or italicized, and followed by a comma; v. = versus: McBoyle, one party, versus (against) the United States of America, the other party	The volume (book) number of the reporter in which the case is printed	The reporter name, abbreviated	The page number[30] on which the opinion begins	Parenthetical information varies depending on the deciding court[31]
McBoyle v. United States,	283	U.S.	25	(1931)
Parties (litigants)	In the library, this is the 283rd *United States Reports* book on the shelf. The book spine will have the number "283."	*McBoyle* opinion is printed in the *United States Reports*, abbreviated U.S.	The *McBoyle* opinion begins on page 25 in volume 283 of the *United States Reports*.	Year of the court's decision

UNITED STATES REPORTS

VOL. 283
OCT. TERM
1930

283 U.S.

A researcher could also simply enter "283 U.S. 25" (with the quotation marks so the terms appear in this exact order) in an online database such as Lexis, Westlaw, or even the internet and find the *McBoyle* written opinion. Citations are unique to each judicial opinion or other source, but there may be more than one case with the same name. Entering "McBoyle v. United States" alone in an online source would give several results, not necessarily the United States Supreme Court *McBoyle* case. But entering the citation alone, "283 U.S. 25," would lead to this 1931 US Supreme Court written opinion in the case. It is therefore preferable to insert the case citation and not just the name when searching for a specific opinion online.

Reporters

Reporters are books that contain certain written judicial opinions. There are different reporters printing decisions for different courts. A case citation has many functions in legal writing, including the identification of the deciding court and attribution to the original source. The following chart lists reporters for federal court decisions:

Court	Reporters and abbreviations	Sample citation (citation form may vary depending on the style manual)
The United States Supreme Court (one court located in Washington, DC)	1. *United States Reports* (U.S.) 2. *Supreme Court Reporter* (S. Ct.) 3. *Lawyer's Edition* (L. Ed. and L. Ed. 2d) (Parallel citations: An opinion will appear in all three of these reporters.)	*McBoyle v. United States*, 283 U.S. 25, 51 S. Ct. 340, 75 L. Ed. 816 (1931) Note: Generally, cite the official citation if available, *United States Reports*, only: *McBoyle v. United States*, 283 U.S. 25 (1931).
Federal appeals courts	*Federal Reporter* F., F.2d, or F.3d (Series: F. is the first series, F.2d is the second series, F.3d is the third series. An opinion will appear in only one of these reporters.)	*McBoyle v. United States*, 43 F.2d 273 (10th Cir. 1930)
Federal district courts	*Federal Supplement* F. Supp., F. Supp. 2d, or F. Supp. 3d (Series: F. Supp. is the first series, F. Supp. 2d is the second series, and F. Supp. 3d is the third series. An opinion will appear in only one of these reporters.)	*United States v. McBoyle*, 200 F. Supp. 219 (W.D. Okla.1927) (fictional citation)

Series: The *2d* and *3d* after a reporter abbreviation refer to a *series*, which is a chronological continuation of the same set of reporters. Lack of a number means it is the first series. For example, for the middle row, in the chart on the previous page, *Federal Reporter*, *F.*, is the first series, cases decided 1880–1924; *F.2d* is the second series, cases decided 1925–93; and *F.3d* is the third series, cases decided 1993 to the present.

A blank in a citation means that a reporter (book) has not yet been printed in hard copy: *Yates v. United States*, 574 U.S. ____, 135 S. Ct. 1074 (2015), will ultimately be printed in volume 574 of the *U.S. Reports*, but since the reporter has not yet been printed (as of the date of this book's publication), there was no page number to cite. However, the *Yates* opinion has already been printed in volume 135 of the *Supreme Court Reporter* and can be found there on page 1074.

Not every judicial opinion will ultimately appear in a reporter. For these *unreported* opinions, there are citations to online databases, such as Lexis (LEXIS) or Westlaw (WL).

EXERCISE 40 | Written Decisions and Level of Court

Instructions: Decide if each of the following statements does or does not describe a judge's written decision. Then, if the statement includes the name of a reporter, identify the level of federal court by referring back to the chart on the previous page.

1. The case was tried in the US District Court for the Southern District of New York:

2. The case is printed in the *Federal Supplement*:

3. The opinion is printed in the *Federal Reporter, Second Series*:

4. The decision is printed in the *United States Reports*:

5. The judge's opinion is that the evidence is inadmissible:

6. The judge's decision is to exclude the evidence:

7. The judge wrote a decision explaining why she excluded the evidence:

WORD STUDY | *Landmark Case, Case/Issue of First Impression, Open Issue, Threshold Issue*

A *landmark* describes something on land that leads people to (marks) a destination. For example, when a boat enters New York Harbor, the Statue of Liberty leads the boat to New York City. The Statue of Liberty is a famous landmark.

A *landmark case* is a significant and historic case that created important rules, in effect leading people to a new understanding of the law. The following are *landmark cases*:

> *Notice that the reporter abbreviation in each of these cases is U.S. This immediately informs the reader that the United States Supreme Court decided these cases, because only United States Supreme Court decisions are printed in the U.S. Reports.*

- *Brown v. Board of Education*, 347 U.S. 483 (1954),* holding that racial segregation in public education is unconstitutional
- *Gideon v. Wainwright*, 372 U.S. 335 (1963), holding that criminal defendants have a constitutional right to counsel in certain criminal proceedings
- *Miranda v. Arizona*, 384 U.S. 436 (1966), mandating that before questioning, law enforcement must inform a person in custody of certain rights, such as the right to remain silent and to have an attorney present during questioning
- *Roe v. Wade*, 410 U.S. 113 (1973), striking down as unconstitutional certain statutes that criminalized abortion
- *National Federation of Independent Business v. Sebelius*, 567 U.S. 519 (2012), upholding the constitutionality of the Affordable Care Act
- *Obergefell v. Hodges*, 576 U.S. ___, 135 S. Ct. 2584 (2015), holding that same-sex marriage is a constitutional right

A *case (issue) of first impression* is a case, or a specific issue in a case, that courts have never addressed. In the digital computer age, there have been many cases of first impression because new technology has raised issues that courts have not previously decided.** For example, courts have recently had to address a novel issue of whether police must obtain a search warrant to obtain records from cell phone towers to prove that a defendant was near certain locations at the times of robberies.

> **To grapple means to struggle with or address a challenge. Courts may grapple with issues of first impression when deciding how constitutional provisions, ratified over 200 years ago, and older laws apply to new technology.*

An *open issue* is an issue that courts have not yet addressed or resolved.

A *threshold issue* is an issue that a court must decide before reaching another issue. For example, before deciding a case *on the merits*, a defendant could argue that the plaintiff does not have standing, or a legally recognized injury. Standing is a *threshold issue* that a court must decide before even considering the case *on the merits*.

threshold

You can't get through the door (and reach the merits) until you pass the threshold.

WORD STUDY | *Line of Cases, Progeny*

A *line of cases* means a series of cases that, in effect, move forward along the same line because they involve a similar issue of law. The rule may evolve through new cases. That is, courts can clarify or modify the rule over time as they address new cases with different facts from the first case in that line.

The line of cases in the following chart shows some ways the *Miranda* rule evolved after the *Miranda* decision: read the excerpts to determine how the line of cases affected or clarified the *Miranda* rule.

1966	1984	2000	2010
A person under custodial interrogation by law enforcement must receive *Miranda* warnings before questioning.	Public safety may excuse the failure to give *Miranda* warnings.	Congress enacted 18 U.S.C. § 3501, changing the *Miranda* rule for a test that a voluntary confession is admissible in court. The US Supreme Court stated that Congress could not legislatively change the *Miranda* rule.	Police informing a defendant "You have the right to talk to a lawyer before answering any of our questions" was insufficient to convey the full force of *Miranda* warnings, which allowed an attorney during the entire interrogation.

line of cases →

Miranda v. Arizona, 384 U.S. 436 (1966)	*New York v. Quarles*, 467 U.S. 649 (1984)	*Dickerson v. United States*, 530 U.S. 428 (2000)	*Florida v. Powell*, 559 U.S. 50 (2010)

Progeny means the outcome or product of something.[32]

Miranda and its *progeny* means *Miranda* and the later cases that are the direct product of *Miranda*, further interpreting the decision.

Types of Appellate Judges' Opinions

A panel of appellate judges is a group of judges deciding one case on appeal in federal or state appellate courts. In an appeals court, there is usually an odd number of judges, such as three or nine, who hear an appeal, so that there is no *tie*. A *tie* in this context is an even number of judges voting against each other, such as 2–2 or 4–4. A tie would prevent a majority (more than half) vote.

For example, in the federal circuits, a panel of three judges decides an appeal, so the majority vote can be 2–1 or 3–0. In the United States Supreme Court, nine justices usually hear a case, and the majority vote can then be 5–4, 6–3, 7–2, 8–1, or 9–0.

Each judge on a panel can choose to vote the same way as the other judges or in different ways from the other judges. An appellate judge can vote in the following ways:

- ▶ Agree with a majority of judges
- ▶ Agree with the majority result but for different reasons
- ▶ Disagree with the majority of judges

Only one judge in the majority then writes the court's majority opinion. The other judges can simply *join* that majority opinion or write a different opinion explaining their vote. In the US Supreme Court, the highest-ranking justice in the majority chooses who writes the opinion. If the chief justice is in the majority, he or she chooses who writes the decision; if the chief justice is in the minority, the most senior justice in the majority decides which justice writes the opinion. *To author* an opinion means to write the opinion, as opposed to simply agreeing with and joining the opinion.

In a trial court, only one judge presides over a trial, and the judge may choose to (or sometimes must) write an opinion in a case describing an issue of law that he or she decided before, during, or after a trial. In a jury trial, a jury votes to decide who wins, but there is no written decision reflecting the reasons for a jury's decision.[33]

The types of opinions that appellate judges can author when they agree with or disagree with the majority are described here:

Types of Appellate Opinions

	Description	Word forms	Words in context
Majority opinion	The opinion that more than half of the judges agree on (at least five of the nine Supreme Court justices or two of the three federal appeals court judges)	Majority (noun, adjective)	Chief Justice Roberts authored the *majority* opinion. Justice Sotomayor *joined* the majority.
Concurring opinion or concurrence, regular concurrence, special concurrence	*Regular concurrence*: An opinion, that a judge chooses to write when voting with the majority as to who wins the case, and agreeing with the court's reasoning *Special concurrence*: An opinion, that a judge writes to explain the reasons for his or her decision when voting with the majority as to who wins the case, but disagreeing with the court's reasoning	To concur (verb); concurring (adjective) opinion (noun); concurrence (noun)	Justice Kagan wrote a *concurrence*. Justice Blackmun *concurred* in the result. Justice O'Connor issued a *concurring* opinion. The *concurring* justices were Justice Kagan, Justice Sotomayor, and Justice Ginsburg.
Dissenting opinion or dissent	An opinion expressing dissent or disagreement with the majority, explaining why one or more judges do not join the majority	To dissent (verb); dissenting (adjective) opinion (noun); dissent (noun)	A *dissenting* opinion was filed by Justice Kennedy. Justice Marshall filed a *dissent*. Justice Thomas *dissented*.

Other Types of Opinions

	Description	Words in context
Plurality	An opinion when there is no majority of judges agreeing as to the reasons why a party should win, but more than half of the judges agree on the result (who wins). In the US Supreme Court, a plurality decision from the nine justices *could be* a 4–1–4 vote or a 3–2–3 vote. In both situations, five votes for the same result determine who wins.	*Yates v. United States*, 135 S. Ct. 1074 (2015), is a *plurality* opinion with a 4–1–4 vote. Five justices agreed on the result, that fish are not "tangible objects" within the meaning of 18 U.S.C. §1519, so there were sufficient votes for Yates (the fisherman) to win. However, one of these five justices wrote a separate concurring opinion giving different reasons from the other four justices as to why fish are not "tangible objects." Four justices dissented.
Per curiam	*Per curiam* means "by the court." The opinion has no single named author and is issued by the court as a whole.	*Roper v. Weaver*, 550 U.S. 598 (2007) is a *per curiam* opinion.

EXERCISE 41 | Describing the Vote of the Appellate Courts

Instructions: Write whether each of the italicized words is a noun, verb, or adjective.

1. Chief Justice Roberts authored the *majority* opinion:

2. Justice Sotomayor *joined* the majority opinion:

3. A *concurrence* was written by Justice Kagan:

4. Justice Kennedy *concurred* in the result:

5. Justice Breyer issued a *concurring* opinion:

6. A *dissenting* opinion was filed by Justice Ginsburg:

7. Justice Thomas *dissented*:

8. Justice Marshall filed a *dissent*:

WORD STUDY | *Recuse*

* US Supreme Court Justice Kagan recused herself from certain cases when she first took the US Supreme Court bench because she was previously involved in the cases as solicitor general.

A judge may *recuse* (excuse) himself or herself and not participate in hearing a case or issuing a decision.* For example, judges who own stock and, therefore, have a financial interest in a corporation that is a party in a case may not be impartial and should recuse themselves from deciding the case.

Both federal and state law contain rules stating when judges are required to, or have the option to, recuse themselves in certain circumstances. In some circumstances, individual judges decides for themselves whether recusal is warranted.

Judicial Ideology

* An independent judiciary is a significant part of the US system of government.

In federal courts, Article III judges serve for life, called *life tenure*, and can therefore make decisions in cases independently and free from political pressure.* That is, they are not elected by constituents and do not fear that they will not be reelected to a court if they make what they believe is the legally correct, but perhaps unpopular, decision in a particular case. Judges strive for objectivity and fairness in their decisions.

But even judges have their own ideologies and ways of interpreting law. As Justice Benjamin Cardozo, former justice of the US Supreme Court, recognized,

> [Judges] may try to see things as objectively as [they] please. Nonetheless, [they] can never see them with any eyes except [their] own. To that test they are all brought [before a judge]—a form of pleading or an act of parliament, the wrongs of paupers or the rights of princes, a village ordinance or a nation's charter.[34]

"Seeing things with their own eyes" may be viewed as deciding cases with conservative or more liberal ways of interpreting laws. Significantly, the lifetime appointment of federal judges shapes the federal judiciary for years to come. A conservative Republican president will probably nominate judges with more conservative judicial ideologies, and a liberal Democratic president will probably nominate judges with more liberal judicial ideologies.

All nine US Supreme Court justices may vote unanimously (9–0) for the same result, or differently, with other possible votes. The expression *swing vote* arises when there is a 5–4 vote—the fifth majority vote determines which way the vote swings. A 5–4 vote may, or may not, split by perceived judicial ideology, and the justice casting the swing vote may vary. The following chart lists the names of the United States

Supreme Court justices in early 2018, before Justice Anthony Kennedy retired from the bench, illustrating a possible swing vote at that time:

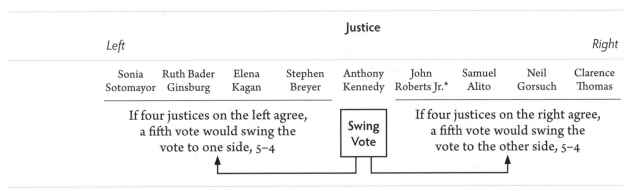

A swing vote determines which side wins when the other justices have split (divided) 4–4.

* *Jr.* is an abbreviation for *Junior*, which indicates that there was a parent with this name, called *Senior* and abbreviated *Sr.* The father of Chief Justice John Roberts Jr. was also called John Roberts and so was known as John Roberts Sr.

Partisanship Revisited

Under the Federal Constitution, Article II, § 2, the Senate gives "advice and consent" to confirm the president's federal judicial nominees. During this process, the Senate holds hearings to vet a federal judge's qualifications. In 2016, the Senate's Republican majority refused to hold a hearing on Democratic then-president Barack Obama's nominee to the Supreme Court of the United States, the chief judge of the federal appeals court for the District of Columbia (DC Circuit), named Merrick Garland.

The Senate Republican majority believed that during a presidential election year, the Senate should hold off the hearings until after that 2016 election, which it did. With a new Republican president in 2016 came a new nominee, now Justice Neil Gorsuch, who was previously a judge on the Tenth Circuit Court of Appeals and is considered to have a more conservative judicial ideology.

In 2018, after Justice Kennedy announced his retirement, there was a partisan battle over Justice Kavanaugh's appointment. A majority of Senate Democrats strongly opposed his confirmation, and a majority of Senate Republicans supported his confirmation. After a long vetting process in the Senate Committee on the Judiciary, the Republican Senate majority voted 50–48 to confirm Justice Kavanaugh.

RESEARCH UPDATE

What is considered to be a more "conservative" judicial ideology, and what is considered to be a more "liberal" judicial ideology?

Why was there a "partisan battle" in the Senate over Justice Kavanaugh's nomination?

What are the names of the justices currently sitting on the US Supreme Court, and which president appointed them?

Who is now the swing vote on the court?

How many votes have been unanimous or near unanimous in the past US Supreme Court term?

How many votes have been 5–4? Have these votes split (divided) by ideology?

Rules and Tests

The term *rule* has many meanings, and one meaning is the sources from a branch of government. Common law rules are one specific type of legal rule. In the context of a civil or a criminal action, the term *rule* can mean "the legal test the court will apply to resolve a legal issue."[35]

In the legal context, this "legal test"[36] will determine who wins. If the plaintiff in a civil case or the prosecution in a criminal case can prove all of the elements[37] or other requirements of the rule, that side wins; if not, that side loses. In judicial opinions, courts may use the terms *rule, test, inquiry, guidepost,* and *framework* to identify a rule. A court might also state the rule in terms of what a party *must prove* or *must establish* or what the court *must determine.*

WORD STUDY | *Carve Out Exceptions to Rules*

Carved out a public safety exception

When courts create exceptions to previously established rules, they *carve out exceptions* to a rule. This expression symbolizes the rule as a solid object, like a rock, with a piece being sculpted or carved out of that rock. This leaves empty spaces or holes, symbolizing the parts of a rule that are being cut out of the original.

Parts of the *Miranda v. Arizona,* 384 U.S. 436 (1966), rule have been carved out of the original rule. The US Supreme Court decided in *New York v. Quarles,* 467 U.S. 649 (1984), that there is a "public safety exception," excusing law enforcement officers from giving *Miranda* warnings when there is a genuine threat to public safety. The defendant in *Quarles* was a suspect in a crime, and police received information that he had a gun. When the police found the suspect, they asked him where the gun was, without giving the *Miranda* warnings. The court *carved out a public safety exception* to this rule concerning when law enforcement must give *Miranda* warnings.

Common Law Rules (Tests)

In a common law system, during the litigation involving a single case, a judge may create, modify, or leave a common law rule as is (without making changes). The following is an example of a common law rule from a state court, New Jersey's top court (its Supreme Court). The plaintiff, Joyce McDougall, was a bystander, watching as the dog of the defendant, Charlotte Lamm, killed McDougall's dog. The following case excerpt states the existing rule, the "legal test" that the court applied:

> [In *Portee v. Jaffee*, . . . and] relying on a decision of the California Supreme Court (*Dillon v. Legg*, 68 Cal. 2d 728, 69 Cal. Rptr. 72, 441 P.2d 912, 920 (1968)), this Court identified four elements that a plaintiff must prove to recover for negligent infliction of emotional distress as a bystander: "(1) the death or serious physical injury of another caused by defendant's negligence; (2) a marital or intimate, familial relationship between plaintiff and the injured person; (3) observation of the death or injury at the scene of the accident; and (4) resulting severe emotional distress." In the three decades since *Portee* was decided, the four-element test has remained in place as the framework for a bystander's emotional distress claim in New Jersey.[38]

In the first sentence, the court informed the reader that this is a common law rule. The *Portee* court relied on a "decision"—*Dillon v. Legg*, from the California Supreme Court—to state the rule, the elements necessary to win when a person claims that he or she suffered "emotional distress as a bystander."[39] It did not identify a part of a constitution, a statute, or an administrative rule allowing a person to recover damages if a person sues for negligent infliction of emotional distress.

Recall that the *elements* of a criminal statute are the statutory requirements that the prosecution must prove in order to win, convicting the defendant of a crime. The *elements* of a common law rule are the common law rule's requirements that a party must prove to win. In *McDougall*, the plaintiff relied on a common law, not a statutory rule, to prove that she was entitled to damages by proving the four elements of the test, because there is no statute in New Jersey stating when a person can recover damages for emotional distress as a bystander for observing the "death or serious physical injury" of another.[40]

This common law rule was not created by the New Jersey legislature, but instead it developed in the courts. It is a common law rule.

Extending Common Law Rules

One of the issues in *McDougall* was whether the New Jersey court should extend the common law rule and allow a person to obtain money damages for negligent infliction of emotional distress after observing the death of a pet. In precedent cases, New Jersey courts had only allowed these claims after the bystander observed injuries to or death of certain (but not all) people. Ultimately, the New Jersey high court decided not to extend the rule to cases in which a person observed the death of a pet.[41]

Codifying Common Law Rules

Legislatures can codify common law rules. For example, after adopting this four-element common law rule, the New Jersey state legislature could codify the rule, that is, pass a law allowing bystanders to recover damages for emotional distress after observing their pet's death. The New Jersey state legislature could adopt the four-element rule as the court stated it or change it.

Under the hierarchy of US law, the statute would then prevail, and New Jersey courts would have to follow the statute, even if the statute is inconsistent with and changed the common law rule. Unless the New Jersey legislature codifies the common law rule, courts throughout New Jersey will apply the *McDougall* rule from New Jersey's high court to determine if bystanders can recover damages for emotional distress observing the death of their pet.

Analyzing Common Law Rules, Which May Differ between Different States

Just like different states may have different statutes from their state legislatures on the same subject, different states may have different common law rules from their state courts on the same subject. In *McDougall*, the court cited precedents from other jurisdictions when deciding not to create a new rule allowing people who observe the death of their pet to recover damages for emotional distress.

The *McDougall* court noted that the following states do not allow recovery:

	The majority of jurisdictions that have considered whether pet owners should be permitted to recover for emotional distress arising from the death of the pet have declined to authorize the cause of action. *See, e.g., Kaufman v. Langhofer*, 223 Ariz. 249,
Arizona	222 P.3d 272, 279 (Ariz. Ct. App. 2009) (holding that "we are unwilling to expand Arizona common law to allow a plaintiff to recover emotional distress or loss of companionship damages for a pet negligently injured or killed"); *Nichols v. Sukaro Kennels*, 555
Iowa	N.W.2d 689, 691–92 (Iowa 1996) (electing to follow majority of jurisdictions in denying
Michigan	recovery for mental distress); *Koester v. VCA Animal Hosp.*, 224 Mich. App. 173, 624
	N.W.2d 209, 211–12 (2000) (declining to recognize cause of action); *Fackler v. Genetzky*,
Nebraska	257 Neb. 130, 595 N.W.2d 884, 892 (1999) (denying recovery for emotional damages
New York	for death of animal); *Jason v. Parks*, 224 A.D.2d 494, 638 N.Y.S.2d 170, 170 (N.Y. App.
Ohio	Div.1996) (same); *Strawser v. Wright*, 88 Ohio App. 3d 751, 610 N.E.2d 610, 612 (1992)
Pennsylvania	(same); *Miller v. Peraino*, 426 Pa. Super. 189, 626 A.2d 637, 640 (1993) (same); *Kondaurov*

Virginia	v. *Kerdasha*, 271 Va. 646, 629 S.E.2d 181, 187 n.4 (2006) (collecting cases that decline to recognize cause of action because animals are deemed personal property); *Pickford*
Washington State	v. *Masion*, 124 Wash. App. 257, 98 P.3d 1232, 1235 (Wash. 2004) (denying recovery for
West Virginia	loss of companionship); *Carbasho v. Musulin*, 217 W. Va. 359, 618 S.E.2d 368, 371 (2005) (denying recovery for emotional damages for death of animal); *Rabideau v. City of*
Wisconsin	*Racine*, 243 Wis. 2d 486, 627 N.W.2d 795, 802 (Wis. 2001) (same).[42]

The *McDougall* court noted that the following states do allow recovery for emotional distress after observing a pet's death:

> Although the great majority of decisions around the country have rejected plaintiffs' requests that they recognize a cause of action for emotional distress based on the death of a pet, a few states have reached the opposite conclusion and have permitted plaintiffs to recover for the emotional distress resulting from the loss of pet. *See*
> Florida   *Knowles Animal Hosp. v. Wills*, 360 So. 2d 37, 38 (Fla. Dist. Ct. App.1978); *Campbell v.*
> Hawaii   *Animal Quarantine Station*, 63 Haw. 557, 632 P.2d 1066, 1071 (1981); *Peloquin v. Calcasieu*
> Louisiana   *Parish Police Jury*, 367 So. 2d 1246, 1251 (La. Ct. App. 1979).[43]

Notice the combinations of numbers and abbreviations in the citations in the preceding quotation. The letters (Haw., P., So., for example) are abbreviations for the names of the reporters printing these state judicial opinions.

Precedent

Precedent is a noun form of the verb *to precede*, meaning "to come before." In the context of judicial decisions, *precedents* are judges' opinions in a civil or criminal case that come before a later case and that a judge in that later case may or must rely on.[44]

Case 1	Case 2
Portee v. Jaffee (1980) A New Jersey case deciding when a bystander can recover damages for negligent infliction of emotional distress as a bystander.	*McDougall v. Lamm* (2012) A New Jersey case, relying on *Portee* as precedent, to decide whether the plaintiff in this later case can recover damages for negligent infliction of emotional distress as a bystander.

Case 1, *Portee* from 1980, precedes or comes before Case 2, *McDougall* from 2012, and is precedent for *McDougall*. The *McDougall* court followed and applied the common law "rule" that the *Portee* court adopted to a different set of facts. *Portee* involved a parent who observed the death of her child, and *McDougall* involved a person who observed the death of her pet.

How Are Common Law Rules and Precedents Related?

In the United States' *common law system*, courts can (1) create common law rules and (2) rely on certain precedents in later cases.

Common law rules are rules from court decisions, as compared with constitutional rules from a constitution, administrative rules from an administrative agency, or statutory rules (the statutes) from a legislature.

Precedents are court decisions that may interpret other sources of law, including but not limited to common law rules as described here:

1. Common law rules	2. Precedents
Rules from court decisions	Previously decided court decisions that a later court cites
	A precedent may interpret and apply one or more of the following:
	1. a constitutional provision
	2. a statute
	3. an executive order or proclamation
	4. an administrative regulation
	5. a common law rule
An example of a common law rule from a judicial opinion:	Examples of precedents: These previously decided cases are precedents that can serve as authority for later court decisions involving similar facts and similar legal issues.
Portee's four-element test to determine if a person can recover for negligent infliction of emotional distress as a bystander, adopted in a court decision. Unless later changed by the New Jersey high court or codified by the New Jersey legislature, New Jersey courts deciding if a person can recover damages for emotional distress after observing the death or injury of another person or pet must apply the *Portee* four-element common law rule (test) to determine who wins.	**1.** *Miranda v. Arizona*, 384 U.S. 436 (1966), interpreting the US Constitution's Fifth Amendment **2.** *McBoyle v. United States*, 283 U.S. 25 (1931), interpreting a federal statute **3.** *Trump v. Hawaii*, 585 U.S. ___, 138 S. Ct. 2392 (2018), interpreting the president's authority to issue a presidential proclamation **4.** *Boreali v. Axelrod*, 71 N.Y. 2d 1 (1987), interpreting the authority of the New York Public Health Council, a New York administrative agency, to issue administrative regulations banning indoor smoking in areas open to the public. **5.** *Portee v. Jaffee*, 84 N.J. 88 (1980), interpreting and adopting a common law rule.

Selected rules:
1. Constitutional rules from a constitution
2. Administrative rules from an administrative agency
3. Statutory rules from a legislature
4. Common law rules from court decisions

In a single case, courts may also create rules to guide later courts in making decisions, even when interpreting statutes from a legislature. For example, Article I, § 8, cl. 8, of the US Constitution authorizes Congress to enact patent statutes as part of federal law. 35 U.S.C. § 101 codifies one aspect of patent law providing, in part, that "[w]hoever invents or discovers any new and useful composition of matter . . . may obtain a patent therefor."

When deciding if something is a "new and useful composition of matter" and is patentable within the meaning of this statute, the US Supreme Court has created further rules including the following (with exceptions as the court noted): "[L]aws of nature, natural phenomena and abstract ideas are not patentable." *Association of Molecular Pathology v. Myriad Genetics, Inc.*, 569 U.S. 576, 589 (2013), quoting *Mayo Collaborative Services v. Prometheus Laboratories, Inc.*, 566 U.S. 66, 70 (2012) (citations omitted). The *Myriad* court applied this rule from precedents. It stated that the "location and order of nucleotides existed in nature before Myriad found them." *Id.* at 590. Though noting that this was an important scientific discovery, the court stated, "we merely hold that genes and the information they encode are not patent eligible under § 101 simply because they have been isolated from the surrounding genetic material." *Id.* at 596. The court discussed and applied the rule from precedent cases—*Mayo* and other cases—when deciding if the patent met the statutory requirements. *Id.* at 589–90. (There were other patent issues raised in this case as well.)

When interpreting statutory terms, courts cannot rewrite or change the statute's terms. However, courts have important powers when deciding cases: to create further rules when interpreting statutes and to determine if the other branches acted consistently with their constitutional powers.

WORD STUDY | *Precedent, Unprecedented, Dangerous Precedent*

Precedent arises in other contexts when something comes before something else: In the newspaper headline "Precedents for Presidents: Bilateral Talks That Made History,"[45] the "Precedents" are presidential meetings with a North Korean leader before 2018 that took place before President Trump and North Korean leader Kim Jong Un met in June 2018.

Unprecedented means something that has never happened before. The meeting between these two leaders was *unprecedented*, because no US president, while in office, had ever met with a North Korean leader.[46]

A *dangerous precedent* is a judicial opinion that could have dangerous consequences for future cases. For example, federal prosecutors have asked judges to order Apple to unlock the iPhones of people who have allegedly committed crimes. Commentators have stated that if a judge ordered Apple to do so, the case would be a *dangerous precedent* because of the dangers to the privacy of all users if judges order Apple to unlock the iPhones of its users. It "could endanger the privacy of all iPhone owners . . . [by] undermin[ing] the very freedoms and liberty our government is meant to protect."[47]

Dispositions: Actions of Appellate Courts

Appellate courts can take certain actions when deciding an appeal:

Affirm, uphold	Reverse, overrule, overturn	Remand	Vacate
A higher court *agrees* with and keeps the same decision as the lower court: same result as in the lower court.	A higher court *disagrees* with and changes the lower court: different result from the lower court.	A higher court sends a case back down to the lower court for additional proceedings. For example, if an appeals court decides that the trial court improperly dismissed a complaint, the court can *reverse* the trial court decision and *remand* (send the case back down) to the trial court for further proceedings.	An award, judgment, or sentence that is *vacated* is set aside or nullified, in effect removing it from existence. Both trial courts and appellate courts can *vacate* an award, a judgment, or a sentence. One example: When a named defendant does not respond to a summons in a lawsuit, a trial court can enter what is called a *default judgment*, or a judgment in plaintiff's favor, by defendant's default or failure to appear. A defendant who later learns about the lawsuit can move to vacate or set aside the default judgment.

An appellate court could do all three of the following acts in a single case:

▸ *Vacate* a judgment
▸ *Reverse*
▸ *Remand*

This means that an appellate court set aside (vacated) the trial court's judgment, disagreed with and changed the trial court's ruling (reversed), and sent the case back to the trial court for further action (remanded).

WORD STUDY | *Judgment, Order*

A *judgment* is "a court's final determination of the rights and obligations of the parties," and an *order* is a court's "written direction or determination," either during or at the end of a case.[48]

A judge may order or require a party to perform an action during (or after) a case, such as turn over documents to the other party during discovery or not discuss the case with newspaper reporters (gag order). A judgment is the ultimate decision on who wins the case: judgment for the plaintiff or judgment for the defendant.

EXERCISE 42 | **Short Opinion from the US Supreme Court**

Instructions: Read the opinion from the United States Supreme Court, and then answer the following questions.

(Slip Opinion)   Cite as: 579 U. S. ____ (2016)

Per Curiam

NOTICE: This opinion is subject to formal revision before publication in the preliminary print of the United States Reports. Readers are requested to notify the Reporter of Decisions, Supreme Court of the United States, Washington, D. C. 20543, of any typographical or other formal errors, in order that corrections may be made before the preliminary print goes to press.

SUPREME COURT OF THE UNITED STATES

No. 15–674

UNITED STATES, ET AL., PETITIONERS *v.* TEXAS, ET AL.*

ON WRIT OF CERTIORARI TO THE UNITED STATES COURT OF APPEALS FOR THE FIFTH CIRCUIT

[June 23, 2016]

PER CURIAM.

The judgment is affirmed by an equally divided Court.

---

* *Et al.* means "and others," referring to "other" parties whose names do not appear here.

1. Who are the parties, and which party filed the cert petition?

2. Did this case originate in (come from) a state court or a federal court?

3. Is there a named author for this opinion? If not, what type of opinion is this called?

4. Did the justices agree with or disagree with the lower court decision?

5. There are nine justices on the Supreme Court. How could the court's vote be "equally divided"?

WORD STUDY | *Overturn, Overrule*

To *overturn* in the following contexts means that a court reversed or changed a lower court ruling or a rule from another branch of government:

▸ The appellate court *overturned* the defendant's conviction (reversed the trial court's ruling).

▸ A federal trial court initially *overturned* President Trump's proclamation banning people from certain countries from entering the United States (found that the proclamation was unconstitutional and therefore invalid). The US Supreme Court ultimately reversed and found the proclamation constitutional.

▸ Congress voted to *overturn* internet privacy rules issued by the Federal Communications Commission, a federal agency (changed rules from an administrative agency).

Overrule in one context means only that a trial judge has ruled on an attorney's objection:

1. During a trial, a judge may either sustain or *overrule* an attorney's objection at a trial.

   • A lawyer asks a question that the other lawyer believes violates the rules governing admissible evidence[49] and says, "I object!" and states the reason for the objection.
   • If the judge agrees and does not allow the witness to answer, the judge says, "sustained" (the judge sustains, or agrees with, the objection).
   • If the judge disagrees with the objection and allows the witness to answer, the judge says, "overruled" (the judge overrules, or disallows, the objection).

2. *Overturn* and *overrule* can be synonyms. Rather than changing the direct result in the same case, a later court may *overturn* or *overrule* (change an earlier rule or principle of law)[50] from its own precedent, as illustrated in the following two examples:

   • The New York Court of Appeals (New York state's top court) *overturned* its own twenty-five-year-old precedent concerning the meaning of parenting.[51]
   • The US Supreme Court changed the *Betts* rule, in *Gideon*, and thereafter required that courts to appoint counsel to represent defendants in certain criminal cases.

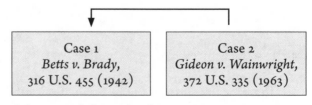

Case 1	Case 2
Betts v. Brady, 316 U.S. 455 (1942)	*Gideon v. Wainwright*, 372 U.S. 335 (1963)

Gideon overruled an earlier decision, *Betts*.

WORD STUDY | *Good Law*

Good law is valid, enforceable law that has not been changed by a governmental body or the courts. Courts have not overruled *Miranda v. Arizona*, 384 U.S. 46 (1966), and it is still good law: law enforcement must still give *Miranda* warnings before a custodial interrogation, subject to exceptions. An overruled court decision, such as *Betts*, is not *good law*; a repealed or an unconstitutional statute is not *good law*; an unconstitutional executive order is not *good law*.

EXERCISE 43 | # Federal, State, or Local: Who Adjudicates?

Background: Congress enacts statutes specifying the subject matter jurisdiction of the federal courts, or when federal courts can adjudicate in specific types of cases based on the US Constitution. Federal district courts have original jurisdiction in certain civil and criminal cases.

State legislatures enact statutes specifying the subject matter jurisdiction of their state and local courts, or when those courts can adjudicate issues of state or local law. Some specialized courts adjudicate specific subjects of law, such as wills (surrogate's courts) or matters related to a family (family courts). There are even specialized parts in some state civil courts handling commercial matters and specialized parts in some state criminal courts hearing drug cases. Courts may have adjudicatory powers based on the amount of monetary damages that a person seeks.

Instructions: This unit describes the structure of federal courts in detail. Now look up the structure of state and local courts. To find a state court's structure, run an internet search by inserting the following terms in an internet search bar:

[Insert state name] court structure chart

For example:

Iowa court structure chart *or* Alaska court structure chart

Find the following states' courts by conducting an internet search, as instructed above, and answer the following questions.

1. What is the name of Iowa's top court?

2. Which Iowa court can adjudicate local city and county ordinances?

3. What is the name of Alaska's high court?

4. Which Alaska courts can hear small claims up to $10,000?

5. What is the name of New York's court of last resort? Does this court have mandatory (appeal by right) or discretionary review?

6. What types of cases can local town and village justice courts adjudicate in New York?

7. What types of cases do family courts hear in New York? Can these courts conduct jury trials? What types of cases do these courts have exclusive jurisdiction over?

8. In Hawaii, which courts have exclusive jurisdiction over small claims up to $5,000?

9. In Hawaii, which courts have exclusive jurisdiction over juvenile claims?

10. What is the name of Hawaii's top court? Does this court have mandatory or discretionary review?

Unit 4 Review

Instructions: Fill in the blanks with the correct words from the word box, making any necessary grammatical changes. You may use a term more than once.

Word Box			
judge	judiciary	adjudicate	judicial
litigate	litigation	proscribe	prescribe

Article III of the United States Constitution establishes the federal _____, consisting of the federal courts. During a civil lawsuit or a criminal prosecution, a _____ interprets the law on a case-by-case basis.

18 U.S.C. § 2312_____ knowingly transporting a stolen "motor vehicle" in interstate commerce. A defendant who is charged with stealing and transporting an inoperable car across state lines could claim that an inoperable car is not a "motor vehicle." The court would interpret § 2312 and the definition of "motor vehicle," which 18 U.S.C. § 2311 _____, in order to decide whether an inoperable car is a "motor vehicle." Because 18 U.S.C. § 2312 is a federal criminal statute, the _____would take place in a federal court; the attorneys would _____ the case, and the judge would _____ the legal issues in the case.

Courts can also decide if a statute is inconsistent with one or more provisions of the Constitution. In *Marbury v. Madison*, 5 U.S. 137 (1803), the United States Supreme Court first articulated the principle that the judiciary has the ultimate responsibility to review and invalidate unconstitutional statutes. _____ review is an important power of the _____ in the US system of checks and balances.

Common law consists of rules that evolve through court decisions, and statutory law is enacted by legislatures.

UNIT 5 Separation of Powers and Checks and Balances

Cases in Context

LESSON 5.1 Overview of the Separation of Powers and Checks and Balances

The framers separated the powers of the three branches of US government. Observe how these articles separated the distinct powers of three branches of federal government:

Article I, Section 1. *The federal legislature*: "All legislative Powers herein granted shall be vested in a Congress of the United States."	Article II, Section 1. *The federal executive*: "The executive Power shall be vested in a President of the United States of America."	Article III, Section 1. *The federal judiciary*: "The judicial Power of the United States shall be vested in one supreme Court, and in such inferior Courts as the Congress may from time to time ordain and establish."

The Founding Fathers separated these powers to ensure that no single branch of government was too powerful. In addition, the framers gave each branch of government the ability to *check*, in effect limit or change, certain actions of the other branches.

Here are some selected checks of the branches of government.

Checking the Legislature

* When a court finds a statute constitutional, it *upholds* the statute. When a court finds a statute unconstitutional, it *strikes down* or *invalidates* the statute.

A judge may invalidate or strike down* a statute from the legislature that is not consistent with the Constitution (constitutional). Two examples: when the legislature does not have the constitutional power to enact that law (as unit 2 explains) or sometimes when a law is inconsistent with a provision in the Bill of Rights. Judges can also determine if the other branches of government exceeded their constitutionally granted powers. The executive can veto laws from the legislature.

Checking the Executive

A judge may find that an executive did not have the power to issue an executive order or proclamation. An executive could overreach, going beyond its powers, by issuing a proclamation or executive order in order to circumvent (go around or avoid) the legislative process when bills cannot pass due to political gridlock. The Federal Constitution, Article II, § 4, prescribes that "the President, Vice-President," and others can be removed from their positions if impeached, and then convicted, for "Treason, Bribery or other high Crimes and Misdemeanors."

Checking the Judiciary

Article II, § 2, vests power in the president to nominate federal judges with the Senate's "advice and consent." The appointment process is a significant power with a long-lasting effect on the judiciary for federal judges with life tenure. Article III, § 1, also states that judges "hold their Offices during good Behaviour," and a judge who does not do so—even a judge with life tenure—can be removed from office. Congress can rewrite certain statutes in response to judicial decisions.

LESSON 5.2 # The Judiciary's Role in the Separation of Powers

The judiciary's separate adjudicatory power is a *check* on the other branches of government. During the adjudication of a civil or criminal case, judges interpret and apply the law. They interpret sources from the other branches of government. Judges will stand by or follow certain judicial precedents, a policy known as *stare decisis*:

> The common law doctrine of stare decisis provides that once a court has decided a legal issue, subsequent cases presenting similar facts should be decided in conformity with the earlier decision.[1]

In *Kimble v. Marvel Entertainment, LLC*, 567 U.S. ___, 135 S. Ct. 2401, 2409 (2015), Justice Kagan, writing for the majority, explained that stare decisis

> "promotes the evenhanded, predictable, and consistent development of legal principles, fosters reliance on judicial decisions, and contributes to the actual and perceived integrity of the judicial process." *Payne v. Tennessee*, 501 U.S. 808, 827–28 (1991). It also reduces incentives for challenging settled precedents, saving parties and courts the expense of endless relitigation.
>
> Respecting *stare decisis* means sticking to some wrong decisions. The doctrine rests on the idea, as Justice Brandeis famously wrote, that it is usually "more important that the applicable rule of law be settled than that it be settled right." *Burnet v. Coronado Oil & Gas Co.*, 285 U.S. 393, 406 (1932) (dissenting opinion). . . . [A]n argument that we got something wrong—even a good argument to that effect—cannot by itself justify scrapping settled precedent. Or otherwise said, it is not alone sufficient that we would decide a case differently now than we did then. To reverse course, we require as well what we have termed a "special justification"—over and above the belief "that the precedent was wrongly decided." *Halliburton Co. v. Erica P. John Fund, Inc.*, 573 U.S. ___, ___, 134 S. Ct. 2398, 2407 (2014).

Higher courts settle the law, and lower courts in the same jurisdiction then follow these rules. But a higher court may, rather than *stand by* a precedent, *overrule* that precedent.[2]

> [Stare decisis] is not an inflexible rule. Judicial decisions simply determine the rights of the parties to an action that is before the court at a particular time in history. They are not, and are not meant to be, immutable laws governing the conduct of mankind and designed for the ages, such as the Ten Commandments. [3]

When courts interpret the law, they may or may not defer to the other branches of government. *To defer*, in this context, means to leave action to another branch of government whether to change the law, out of respect for that other branch's constitutional power.*

* To deter, by contrast, means to incentivize people not to take certain actions. The potential for criminal punishment, such as jail, may deter people from committing crimes.

When a court interprets the Constitution, it will be "more prone to correct an error stemming from an earlier decision"[4] because the judiciary has the ultimate duty to decide the constitutionality of statutes under a principle called *judicial review*.

By contrast, when a court decides whether to overrule a precedent interpreting a statute, a court might defer to the legislature, which has constitutional legislative powers, and can amend the statute itself. "[U]nlike in a constitutional case, critics of [US Supreme Court] ruling[s] [interpreting federal statutes] can take their objections across the street, and Congress can correct any mistake it sees." *Kimble v. Marvel Entertainment, LLC*, 135 S. Ct. at 2409 (citation omitted).

Since courts create common law rules, they cannot defer to the other branches of government to change perceived errors in precedents. How does stare decisis affect a court's decision to stand by its past precedents when interpreting common law rules? Read the case summaries in the next lesson, in which courts interpreted common law rules, for the answer.

IT IS EMPHATICALLY THE PROVINCE AND DUTY OF THE JUDICIAL DEPARTMENT TO SAY WHAT THE LAW IS.

MARBURY v. MADISON

1803

Judicial review under *Marbury v. Madison*, 5 U.S. 137 (1803). Plaque on the wall inside the US Supreme Court Building in Washington, DC.

LESSON 5.3 Cases in Context

This lesson examines selected court decisions illustrating how the judiciary has interpreted laws from the three branches of government. The case summaries are titled "Separation of Powers" to highlight the roles of the three branches of government in each case, when applicable.

Interpreting Statutes

The judiciary can determine if Congress exceeded its Article I, § 8, enumerated powers when passing laws. Chief Justice Roberts stated that courts are generally "reticen[t] to invalidate the acts of the Nation's elected leaders,"[5] whom the citizens of the United States have elected to represent them.

> "Proper respect for a co-ordinate branch of the government" requires us to strike down an Act of Congress only if "the lack of constitutional authority to pass [the] act in question is clearly demonstrated." *United States v. Harris*, 106 U.S. 629, 635 (1883). Members of this Court are vested with the authority to interpret the law; we possess neither the expertise nor the prerogative to make policy judgments. Those decisions are entrusted to our Nation's elected leaders, who can be thrown out of office if the people disagree with them. It is not our job to protect the people from the consequences of their political choices.[6]

In the following case 1, the United States Supreme Court upheld a statute, holding that Congress had the Article I, § 8, power to enact the statute. In case 2, the United States Supreme Court struck down a statute, holding that Congress did not have an Article I, § 8, power to enact the statute.

Case 1: *National Federation of Independent Business v. Sebelius*, 567 U.S. 519 (2012)

This case interprets the legislature's Article I, § 8, enumerated powers in the Federal Constitution when enacting a federal statute.

Background

Congress enacted the Affordable Care Act (ACA)[7] in 2010. One part of this federal statute required that many Americans have certain health insurance coverage. The plaintiffs—business organization and others—claimed that Congress did not have the Article I, § 8, power to pass the law.

The National Federation of Independent Business (NFIB) and others brought suit against Kathleen Sebelius, then secretary of Health and Human Services (HHS), requesting that the court *strike down*, or invalidate, the law.

One Issue in the Case

Did the legislature exceed its constitutionally granted Article I, § 8, power when enacting that law? In this landmark 2012 case, the US Supreme Court both analyzed the power of Congress to enact a federal law and reviewed the balance of power between federal and state governments.

Holding

The statute is constitutional. Congress had the Article I, § 8, power to enact the law under the taxing clause but not under the commerce clause or the necessary and proper clause.

Separation of Powers

- Despite partisanship, there were enough votes from both Democrats and Republicans in both houses of Congress to pass the law in 2010.
- President Obama, a Democrat, signed the bill into law in order to extend health insurance to more people throughout the United States.
- The Department of Health and Human Services (HHS), the administrative agency responsible for administering (carrying out) health care policy, and the Internal Revenue Service (IRS) promulgated rules to implement Obamacare. The IRS regulates federal tax payments, and nonexempt people had to pay a penalty, when paying federal taxes, if they did not have the required health insurance.
- Multiple plaintiffs brought suit in various federal courts:

  - The National Federation of Business, individuals affected by the law, and twenty-six states brought suit in the United States District Court for the Northern District of Florida. The Court of Appeals for the Eleventh Circuit reviewed the case upon appeal, affirming the lower court and reversing the lower court in certain aspects of the decision.

- Other plaintiffs brought suit in other federal courts, and other federal courts of appeals heard the cases in the Sixth Circuit, Fourth Circuit, and DC Circuit.

▶ The United States Supreme Court granted certiorari in 2012 and heard the case, upholding the law by a 5–4 vote (under the taxing power).[8]

▶ In 2017, a new Republican president was elected, and there were Republican majorities in both houses of Congress.

▶ The Republican-controlled Congress passed a new tax law, eliminating the penalty for failure to have required health insurance coverage.

RESEARCH UPDATE

How many Republicans and how many Democrats voted to repeal the individual mandate in 2017 votes? Was this a partisan vote?

Has Congress repealed or further amended Obamacare since 2017?

Case 2: *United States v. Lopez*, 514 U.S. 549 (1995)

This case interprets the legislature's Article I, § 8, enumerated powers in the Federal Constitution when enacting a federal statute.

Background

Congress enacted the Gun-Free School Zones Act, criminalizing the possession of a firearm within 1,000 feet of a school (18 U.S.C. § 922(q)(1)(A) (1988 ed., Supp. V)). A federal grand jury indicted* Alfonso Lopez Jr., a twelfth-grade student in Texas, under this statute for bringing a concealed weapon to school. At trial, Lopez's attorney claimed that the statute was unconstitutional because the law exceeded the scope of Congress's Article I, § 8, commerce clause power.

At the time of Lopez's indictment, 18 U.S.C. § 922(q)(1)(A) provided as follows: "It shall be unlawful for any individual knowingly to possess a firearm at a place that the individual knows, or has reasonable cause to believe, is a school zone."[9]

*Issued an *indictment*. See "Comparing Terminology in Civil and Criminal Cases" in lesson 4.2.

Holding

The statute is unconstitutional. Congress did not have the power to enact this law under its Article I, § 8, cl. 3, commerce clause power.

Separation of Powers

▶ Congress enacted 18 U.S.C. § 922(q)(1)(A).

▶ President George H. W. Bush signed the bill into law.

- ▶ Federal prosecutors (US attorney in the state of Texas in the Department of Justice) charged Alfonso Lopez with violating this federal law.
- ▶ A grand jury, representatives from the community, indicted Lopez, deciding that the evidence that the prosecutor presented to them was sufficient to hold him over for trial.
- ▶ The judge convicted the defendant, Lopez, after a bench trial in the United States District Court for the Western District of Texas. Although the US Supreme Court ultimately decided differently, the trial judge initially decided that the Gun Free School Zones Act was a constitutional exercise of Congress's Article I, § 8, commerce clause power.
- ▶ The defendant-appellant Lopez appealed his conviction to the United States District Court for the Fifth Circuit, which reversed the conviction, holding that Congress did not have the Article I, § 8, power to enact this law.
- ▶ The prosecution-petitioner, the United States of America, appealed the Fifth Circuit decision, filing a petition for a writ of certiorari. The United States Supreme Court granted cert, and in a 5–4 decision, affirmed the Fifth Circuit's decision. Lopez's conviction was vacated because the statute by which he was charged was unconstitutional; Congress exceeded its power in enacting the statute.
- ▶ In response to the US Supreme Court decision invalidating the statute, Congress thereafter amended the Gun-Free School Zone Act in 1997, adding an element to the offense, which requires that the firearm has moved in interstate commerce. The current law, 18 U.S.C. § 922(q)(2)(A), states, "It shall be unlawful for any individual knowingly to possess a firearm that has moved in or that otherwise affects interstate or foreign commerce at a place that the individual knows, or has reasonable cause to believe, is a school zone."

RESEARCH UPDATE

There have been additional constitutional challenges to this new, amended statute and calls by a president to repeal the law. Have these challenges succeeded, or is this statute still "good law"?

Case 3: *McBoyle v. United States*, 283 U.S. 25 (1931)

This case interprets one specific statutory term. There was no challenge to the federal legislature's initial power to enact the law.

Background
A jury convicted William McBoyle of violating a federal statute, the National Motor Vehicle Theft Act, 18 U.S.C. § 408, for knowingly transporting a stolen airplane across state lines.

At the time of McBoyle's conviction, the statute, 18 U.S.C. § 408(2)(a), defined "motor vehicle" as follows: "The term 'motor vehicle' shall include an automobile, automobile truck, automobile wagon, motor cycle, or any other self-propelled vehicle not designed for running on rails."

Issue
Is an airplane a "self-propelled vehicle" within the meaning of the statute?

Holding
No. An airplane is not a "motor vehicle" within the meaning of this statute, as it is not "an automobile, motorcycle, or a self-propelled vehicle not designed for running on rails"; it is a machine that flies in the air.

The court stated that airplanes existed in 1919 when Congress enacted the statute, and if Congress had wanted to include airplanes within the proscription of this statute, it would have done so (H.R. Rep. No. 66-312, at 1 (1919)). It is Congress's job to legislate, and the legislative history from Congress (see the House report in lesson 2.4) made no reference to airplanes, only cars and automobiles.

Separation of Powers
- ▸ The House of Representatives Committee on the Judiciary issued a report (see the House report in lesson 2.4) identifying the need for federal legislation after thieves began stealing vehicles and moving them from one state to another (in interstate commerce) to avoid prosecution.
- ▸ Congress passed 18 U.S.C. § 408.
- ▸ The president did not sign the law or veto it within the time prescribed in the Constitution (Article I, § 7), and it became a law (see the *Statutes at Large* in lesson 2.4).
- ▸ Federal law enforcement officials investigated the theft of an airplane, which moved interstate from Illinois to Oklahoma.
- ▸ Federal prosecutors charged McBoyle with violating 18 U.S.C.§ 408(3) for this theft; McBoyle paid another person to transport the plane interstate.
- ▸ The feds ultimately found the airplane in Oklahoma after it had crossed state lines, and the trial therefore took place in the United States District Court for the Western District of Oklahoma. A jury at trial convicted McBoyle of violating 18 U.S.C. § 408.
- ▸ McBoyle appealed his conviction, and the United States Court of Appeals for the Tenth Circuit affirmed the conviction, holding also that an airplane was a "motor vehicle" within the meaning of the statute.
- ▸ McBoyle petitioned the United States Supreme Court for a writ of certiorari, and the court granted the cert petition, agreeing to hear the case. The Supreme Court reversed, vacating McBoyle's conviction and holding that an airplane is not a "motor vehicle" within the meaning of the statute.
- ▸ After the US Supreme Court decision in *McBoyle*, Congress amended (rewrote) the National Motor Vehicle Theft Act in response to the court's decision.

Compare the two versions of the statute:

1. The original *statutory language* (text) of the National Motor Vehicle Theft Act (18 U.S.C. § 408(3)): "Whoever shall transport or cause to be transported in interstate or foreign commerce a motor vehicle, knowing the same to have been stolen, shall be punished by a fine of not more than $5,000, or by imprisonment of not more than five years, or both." 18 U.S.C. § 408(2)(a) defined "motor vehicle" to "include an automobile, automobile truck, automobile wagon, motor cycle, or any other self-propelled vehicle not designed for running on rails."

2. The amended *statutory language* (text) of the National Motor Vehicle Theft Act, after *McBoyle* (18 U.S.C. § 2312): "Whoever transports in interstate or foreign commerce a motor vehicle, vessel, or aircraft, knowing the same to have been stolen, shall be fined under this title or imprisoned not more than 10 years, or both." 18 U.S.C. § 2311 included this definition: "'Aircraft' means any contrivance now known or hereafter invented, used, or designed for navigation of or for flight in the air."

RESEARCH UPDATE

Statutory construction or interpretation tools, such as *plain meaning, legislative history*, and others, guide courts in interpreting statutes. The *McBoyle* court used several construction tools to interpret this statute. Read more about these tools in both the federal appeals court decision, 43 F.2d 273 (10th Cir. 1930), and the U.S. Supreme Court decision, 283 U.S. 25 (1931).

There are many articles and books that summarize statutory construction tools, such as a comprehensive book by Antonin Scalia and Bryan A. Garner, *Reading Law: The Interpretation of Legal Texts* (Eagan, MN: Thomson West, 2012).

WORD STUDY | ## A Broad Reading of a Statute, a Narrow (Strict) Reading of a Statute

The expressions *broad reading* or *narrow (strict) reading* of law describe how courts may interpret a particular law. With respect to a statute, a *broad reading* means that courts read (interpret) the statute in an expansive way by including many different applications. A *narrow (strict) reading* of a statute means that courts interpret a statute in a very limited way.

For example, a broad reading of the 18 U.S.C. § 408(2)(a) definition of "motor vehicle" would have included an expansive list of possible vehicles, including airplanes, farm equipment not used to transport people, inoperable cars, or even car parts. A narrow reading would limit the term "motor vehicle" to include only operable cars that may transport people on land.

Interpreting Executive Orders and Proclamations

The executive carries out the law and creates policy through executive orders and proclamations. During litigation, a court can check the executive's power in order to ensure that the president does not overreach and has either the constitutional or statutory authority to act. Courts can also determine if administrative agencies have overstepped their authority when promulgating rules.

Case 1: *Youngstown Sheet & Tube Co. v. Sawyer*, 343 U.S. 579 (1952)

This case interprets the president's power to issue an executive order.

Background
In 1952, President Truman issued Executive Order 10340, directing the secretary of commerce to take possession of certain steel mills in order to avert a strike (workers refusing to work). The president asserted that he had authority to do so, in part, as commander in chief of the armed forces under Article II of the US Constitution.

Issue
Did the president have the constitutional power to issue this executive order to take over a private business?

Holding
No. "The President's power, if any, to issue the order must stem either from an act of Congress or from the Constitution itself. There is no statute that expressly authorizes the President to take possession of property as he did here. Nor is there any act of Congress to which our attention has been directed from which such a power can fairly be implied." *Youngstown Sheet & Tube Co. v. Sawyer*, 343 U.S. 579, 585 (1952).

Separation of Powers
▸ Employees of a steel mill decided to strike (refuse to work), seeking more money from their employer.
▸ After varied efforts to avoid a strike failed, the president of the United States issued an executive order directing the secretary of commerce to take over the plaintiff-company in order to continue to produce steel. Notice the defendant's name, Sawyer; Charles Sawyer was then secretary of commerce, the head of the agency that the president directed to carry out the executive order.
▸ The company brought suit in the United States District Court for the District of Columbia, challenging the executive action as unconstitutional executive overreach. The trial court issued an injunction prohibiting the government from taking over the steel mill.

- ▶ The United States Court of Appeals for the DC Circuit stayed (stopped enforcement of) the injunction.
- ▶ The United States Supreme Court granted certiorari and affirmed the Court of Appeals' decision. The court noted that Article I vests legislative powers in Congress, and the president can only veto laws. Taking over a private business under executive power was unprecedented and was not authorized by any statute or constitutional provision.

Historical Note

Consider the year of a decision when reading cases: "Judicial decisions simply determine the rights of the parties to an action that is before the court at a particular time in history."[10]

In 1952, the United States was involved in the Korean War, and the president, as commander in chief, believed that steel production was necessary to further the United States' war effort. The United States Supreme Court recognized that, even in the context of a war, the separation of powers required the court to invalidate President Truman's executive order: "The Founders of this Nation entrusted the lawmaking power to the Congress alone in both good and bad times. It would do no good to recall the historical events, the fears of power and the hopes for freedom that lay behind their choice. Such a review would but confirm our holding that this seizure order cannot stand." *Youngstown Sheet & Tube Co. v. Sawyer*, 343 U.S. 579, 589 (1952).

Case 2: *Trump v. Hawaii*, 585 U.S. ___, 138 S. Ct. 2392 (2018)

This case interprets the president's power to issue a proclamation. The justices' 5–4 vote split along ideological lines.

Background

In 2017, President Trump issued two separate executive orders temporarily banning certain foreign nationals from entering the United States. The government sought to ban entrants until a procedure for extreme vetting (very careful review) would protect the United States from terrorists entering into the country. On September 24, 2017, the president issued an order resulting in a travel ban as Proclamation 9465,[11] to prohibit entrants from seven countries until adequate vetting procedures would ensure that these nationals are not risks to the United States' security.

Issue

One question presented was "whether the President had authority under the [Immigration and Nationality, 8 U.S.C. § 1182(f)] Act to issue the Proclamation."[12]

Presidential Proclamation Enhancing Vetting Capabilities and Processes
for Detecting Attempted Entry into the United States by Terrorists or
Other Public-Safety Threats

[T]he Secretary of Homeland Security, in consultation with the Secretary of State and the Attorney General, has determined that a small number of countries—out of nearly 200 evaluated—remain deficient at this time with respect to their identity-management and information-sharing capabilities, protocols, and practices. In some cases, these countries also have a significant terrorist presence within their territory.

As President, I must act to protect the security and interests of the United States and its people. I am committed to our ongoing efforts to engage those countries willing to cooperate, improve information-sharing and identity-management protocols and procedures, and address both terrorism-related and public-safety risks. Some of the countries with remaining inadequacies face significant challenges. Others have made strides to improve their protocols and procedures, and I commend them for these efforts. But until they satisfactorily address the identified inadequacies, I have determined, on the basis of recommendations from the Secretary of Homeland Security and other members of my Cabinet, to impose certain conditional restrictions and limitations, as set forth . . . in section 2 of this proclamation.

NOW, THEREFORE, I, DONALD J. TRUMP, by the authority vested in me by the Constitution and the laws of the United States of America, including sections 212(f) and 215(a) of the Immigration and Nationality Act (INA), 8 U.S.C. 1182(f) and 1185(a), and section 301 of title 3, United States Code, hereby find that, absent the measures set forth in this proclamation, the immigrant and nonimmigrant entry into the United States of persons described in section 2 of this proclamation would be detrimental to the interests of the United States, and that their entry should be subject to certain restrictions, limitations, and exceptions.[13]

Holding

In *Hawaii v. Trump*, 878 F.3d 662 (9th Cir. 2017), the Ninth Circuit Court of Appeals held that the president exceeded his authority to control immigration, granted to him by Congress in the Immigration and Nationality Act, 8 U.S.C. § 1182, when issuing this proclamation, violating the separation of powers.

In 2018, the United States Supreme Court (5–4) reversed the Ninth Circuit, upholding the president's authority to issue this proclamation. The case name changed order to *Trump v. Hawaii* in the United States Supreme Court because President Trump lost the case in the Ninth Circuit and filed the petition for certiorari. The order of the names in the case changes in the United States Supreme Court when the original plaintiff lost in the court below and is the party seeking review or filing the petition.

Interpreting Common Law Rules

Courts may create common law rules through their written opinions. Since courts create these rules, they cannot defer to other branches when deciding whether to stand by precedents.

However, in the area of personal injury in torts especially, courts may be more flexible in changing rules than in real property, wills, and commercial transactions.[14] Lawyers, businesses, and others may rely on rules that courts create when writing a real estate contract or a will or forming a commercial transaction, and there is a need for "stability and predictability," which would be compromised if rules were changed "in the middle of the game."[15]

The following two opinions interpret common law rules; there is no constitutional provision, statute, executive order, or administrative rule. Case 1 illustrates a court deciding whether to extend a common law rule in a tort. Case 2 illustrates a court interpreting the validity of a contract provision. There are numerous other types of common law rules that courts interpret.

Case 1: *McDougall v. Lamm*, 211 N.J. 203 (2012)

This case involves a court's interpretation of a common law rule.

Background

A woman watched (was a bystander) when another dog killed the woman's dog. She sued the dog's owner, in part for a type of action called the *negligent infliction of emotional distress*, a tort (civil wrong) containing the following elements: "(1) the death or serious physical injury of another caused by defendant's negligence; (2) a marital or intimate, familial relationship between plaintiff and the injured person; (3) observation of the death or injury at the scene of the accident; and (4) resulting severe emotional distress." *McDougall v. Lamm*, 211 N.J. 203, 214–15 (2012), quoting *Portee v. Jaffee*, 84 N.J. 88, 101 (1980).

Issue

Can a person have an "intimate familial relationship" satisfying element 2 of this statute and allowing a bystander to recover damages for negligent infliction of emotional distress after observing the pet's death?

Holding

No. A person cannot have a "marital or intimate familial relationship" with a pet and therefore cannot recover emotional distress damages under this common law rule. The court noted that pets are traditionally considered property, and although some states do permit people to recover damages for negligent infliction of emotional distress for the loss of a pet, New Jersey's top court refused to do so and would not extend the common law rule to include the loss of a pet. This rule does not allow all *people* to recover damages after observing the death of another person. The court noted that extending this rule to nonhumans could result in many new and potentially unverifiable claims, even some involving destruction of property.[16]

In *McDougall*, the defendant argued that "it would set a dangerous precedent to expand the scope of bystander liability to non-humans." *McDougall*, 211 N.J. at 210. Do you agree?

Separation of Powers

Since this decision is based on a common law rule, the relevant actions took place in court:

- ▶ Various state courts developed the common law four-element test for the tort of negligent infliction of emotional distress that applies in each state. New Jersey's rule is quoted on the previous page. According to the *McDougall* court, two other states—Illinois and Tennessee—do have statutes authorizing this cause of action. *McDougall*, 211 N.J. at 221–22, n. 2.
- ▶ The plaintiff, Joyce McDougall, sued the defendant, Charlotte Lamm, in a New Jersey court, asserting that she is entitled to recover damages for negligent infliction of emotional distress under this tort.
- ▶ There was a bench trial in a New Jersey trial court after both parties waived their right to a jury trial. The trial judge dismissed the emotional distress claim but allowed a negligence claim to proceed and awarded $5,000 in compensatory damages to the plaintiff on negligence grounds.
- ▶ The New Jersey Appellate Division affirmed the trial court's decision.
- ▶ New Jersey's top court, the Supreme Court of New Jersey, affirmed the decision.
- ▶ Could the plaintiff appeal from New Jersey's Supreme Court to the United States Supreme Court? The answer is no. Since there is no federal issue involved and the parties are both New Jersey residents, the United States Supreme Court could not hear the case, and the plaintiff cannot appeal any further. New Jersey's court of last resort issued a final decision in the matter, and all New Jersey courts must follow this precedent in later cases.
- ▶ The New Jersey legislature could choose to codify this rule but had not done so at the time of this decision.

WORD STUDY | *Bright Line Rule*

A *bright line rule* is a rule that is intended to be very clear or bright, so people can clearly and easily follow the rule. If there is a bright line rule, judges have clear guidelines and little discretion when applying the rule to a given case.

For example, *McDougall* favored a clear, *bright line rule* stating that a person cannot recover for negligent infliction of emotional distress as a bystander after observing the death of any kind of pet. The rule is clear and bright because it is easy to see and follow; and judges have little discretion in applying the rule. A judge does not have to decide whether a person who observes the death of different kinds of pets can or cannot recover damages for negligent infliction of emotional distress.

Case 2: *Pure Power Boot Camp, Inc. v. Warrior Fitness, LLC,* 813 F. Supp. 2d 489 (S.D.N.Y. 2011)

This case interprets a common law contract rule governing the validity of a restrictive covenant in a contract.

Background

The plaintiff was a fitness company, which sued multiple defendants including former employees. Before working at the company, the defendants agreed to a restrictive covenant (also called a *noncompete* or *covenant not to compete*) in their employment contract, not to compete with the fitness company for ten years after they left the plaintiff's employment. However, the defendants left the plaintiff's fitness center and opened a club, which was very similar to the plaintiff's.

The plaintiffs sued the defendants on many grounds, including both state and federal claims seeking damages from the defendants. The defendants counterclaimed, in turn, suing the plaintiff in the same lawsuit, claiming the plaintiff violated certain laws.

Issue

One issue is this case was whether the noncompete covenant was reasonable and therefore enforceable.

Holding

The noncompete agreement in this case was unreasonable and therefore unenforceable. State law governs the enforceability of noncompete agreements, and these laws vary from state to state. Some states legislatures have enacted statutes prohibiting or limiting the enforceability of noncompete agreements, and others have not. New York does not have a general statute banning noncompete agreements but does prohibit them in certain areas, such as the broadcasting industry.[17] Instead, New York applies a common law rule of "reasonableness" that has developed through court decisions. *Pure Power*, 813 F. Supp. 2d at 506, quoting *Ticor Title Ins. Co. v. Cohen*, 173 F.3d 63, 70 (2d Cir. 1999). Here are the elements of this test: specifically, an agreement not to compete in New York will be enforced only if "it is reasonable in time and area, necessary to protect the employer's legitimate interests, not harmful to the general public, and not unreasonably burdensome to the employee." *Reed, Roberts Assoc. v. Strauman*, 40 N.Y.2d 303, 307 (1976).

Citing two other precedents from New York in which courts found ten-year restrictions in employment contracts unreasonable in time and area, the *Pure Power* court also held that the ten-year and, in effect, worldwide restriction was unreasonable and therefore unenforceable.

Separation of Powers

Since this case involved a common law rule, all relevant proceedings took place in the courts.

▸ Various state courts developed the common law test for the enforceability of a non-compete agreement in an employment contract. New York's rule is quoted on the previous page.

▸ The plaintiff, Pure Power, sued the defendants for violating the noncompete agreement, originally filing the lawsuit in a New York state court.

▸ The defendants counterclaimed, alleging violations of New York and federal law, and removed the case to the federal court, the United States District Court for the Southern District of New York. The federal court had subject matter jurisdiction in the case because there were allegations that the parties violated federal statutes.

▸ The parties agreed to have a bench trial, and the judge decided the case, ultimately awarding damages to the plaintiff on various grounds. However, the court dismissed the plaintiff's claim regarding the noncompete agreement.

▸ Neither party appealed, and the trial court's decision is final.

▸ The New York state legislature could choose to codify this rule but had done so at the time of this decision.

Unit 5 Review

Instructions: In the following cases, the court either stood by or overruled a precedent. Look up each case, and then answer the following questions.

Case 1: *Kimble v. Marvel Entertainment, LLC,* 567 U.S. ____, 135 S. Ct. 2401 (2015).
Case 2: *Roper v. Simmons,* 543 U.S. 551 (2005).
Case 3: *South Dakota v. Wayfair,* 585 U.S. ____, 138 S. Ct. 2080 (2018).
Case 4: *Obergefell v. Hodges,* 576 U.S. ____, 135 S. Ct. 2584 (2015).
Case 5: *Planned Parenthood of Southeastern Pennsylvania v. Casey,* 505 U.S. 833 (1992).

1. What was the name of the case that the court was deciding to either stand by or overrule?

2. What did the Court decide?

3. Which source of law was the Court interpreting?

4. If the Court was interpreting a statute from the legislature, did the Court defer to the legislature to change the law rather than overrule the precedent itself?

Appendix 1

Selected Provisions of the US Bill of Rights

The Bill of Rights consists of the first ten amendments to the US Constitution and contains many important restrictions on government action, such as enacting laws "prohibiting the free exercise" of religion or "abridging the freedom of speech." U.S. Const. amend. I.

Here is the preamble to the Bill of Rights and selected provisions from the Bill of Rights (ratified in 1791), as well as the Fourteenth Amendment (ratified in 1868). The Fourteenth Amendment is a significant post–Civil War amendment. It added several provisions, including when a person is a citizen of the United States.

Preamble

Congress of the United States begun and held at the City of New York, on Wednesday the fourth of March, one thousand seven hundred and eighty nine. The Conventions of a number of the States, having at the time of their adopting the Constitution, expressed a desire, in order to prevent misconstruction or abuse of its powers, that further declaratory and restrictive clauses should be added: And as extending the ground of public confidence in the Government, will best ensure the beneficent ends of its institution.

Amendment I

Congress shall make no law respecting an establishment of religion, or prohibiting the free exercise thereof; or abridging the freedom of speech, or of the press; or the right of the people peaceably to assemble, and to petition the Government for a redress of grievances.

Amendment II

A well regulated Militia, being necessary to the security of a free State, the right of the people to keep and bear Arms, shall not be infringed.

Amendment IV

The right of the people to be secure in their persons, houses, papers, and effects, against unreasonable searches and seizures, shall not be violated, and no Warrants shall issue, but upon probable cause, supported by Oath or affirmation, and particularly describing the place to be searched, and the persons or things to be seized.

Amendment V

No person shall be held to answer for a capital, or otherwise infamous crime, unless on a presentment or indictment of a Grand Jury, except in cases arising in the land or naval forces, or in the Militia, when in actual service in time of War or public danger; nor shall any person be subject for the same offence to be twice put in jeopardy of life or limb; nor shall be compelled in any criminal case to be a witness against himself, nor be deprived of life, liberty, or property, without due process of law; nor shall private property be taken for public use, without just compensation.

Amendment VI

In all criminal prosecutions, the accused shall enjoy the right to a speedy and public trial, by an impartial jury of the State and district wherein the crime shall have been committed, which district shall have been previously ascertained by law, and to be informed of the nature and cause of the accusation; to be confronted with the witnesses against him; to have compulsory process for obtaining witnesses in his favor, and to have the Assistance of Counsel for his defence.

Amendment VII

In Suits at common law, where the value in controversy shall exceed twenty dollars, the right of trial by jury shall be preserved, and no fact tried by a jury, shall be otherwise re-examined in any Court of the United States, than according to the rules of the common law.

Amendment VIII

Excessive bail shall not be required, nor excessive fines imposed, nor cruel and unusual punishments inflicted.

Amendment X

The powers not delegated to the United States by the Constitution, nor prohibited by it to the States, are reserved to the States respectively, or to the people.

"XIV," below, are Roman numerals for the number 14. Notice the Fourteenth Amendment's wording below: "No State shall make or enforce any law." Under the "incorporation doctrine," the US Supreme Court has held that, through the Fourteenth Amendment, many, but not all, of the first ten amendments in the Bill of Rights apply to the states and not just to the federal government.

Amendment XIV

All persons born or naturalized in the United States, and subject to the jurisdiction thereof, are citizens of the United States and of the State wherein they reside. No State shall make or enforce any law which shall abridge the privileges or immunities of citizens of the United States; nor shall any State deprive any person of life, liberty, or property, without due process of law.

Appendix 2

Idioms, Phrasal Verbs, and Other Terms (Selected Meanings)

Bitter battle

Bitter means sharp or strong, as in food such as a lemon that has a sharp and strong flavor. A *battle* is a fight.

> There was a *bitter battle* in Congress over whether to confirm the president's judicial nominee.

Blow up

To destroy, as with explosives or in a symbolic meaning

> The engineer used explosives to *blow up* the building.

To get very angry

> The employer *blew up* when he discovered that his former employee was doing business with the employer's customers in violation of the covenant not to compete.

Blown away

To be affected or surprised in a positive way.

> The student was *blown away* by her excellent grades.

Call on, cold call, on call

Call on and cold call: Ask someone to answer a question, without asking for a volunteer

On call: Know in advance you will have to answer questions

> Be prepared for class. If the professor *calls on* you, you must answer the question.

> In some classes, professors *cold call*; students do not know in advance if they will be *called on* to answer questions.

> In other classes, professors do not *call on* you. They will instead tell students that they will be *on call* on a specific day. You will have to answer questions on that specific day.

Contract out*

Give a contract to someone to perform services

> The company *contracted out* its security services to a private firm.

* Distinguish *contract out* from the colloquial expression *to put a contract out*. In some crime movies, one might hear that someone was hired to murder, or *put a contract out* on, another person.

Day off, off day

Day off: Vacation day

> You will have a *day off* on the Labor Day holiday in September because there are no classes.

Off day: A nonwork day or a day when things are not going well for an individual

Nonwork day:
> On the lawyer's *off days*, she did pro bono work in which she volunteered and did not charge the clients for her time.

Things are not going well:
> I was having an *off day*: I missed the subway by two seconds, spilled my coffee, and arrived late to class.

Find out	**Receive a decision about, discover** After two weeks, the student *found out* that she got the job she had applied for. **Learn how to (colloquial)** It took much time to *find out* how to read US case law.
Get it	**To understand** After a complicated lecture, the student said, "I don't *get it*."
Hit the books	**Go to study** Law students *hit the books* every day to stay current with their work.
Let go	**Fire from a job** Due to reduced demand, the employer *let* one hundred employees *go* (or *let go* of one hundred employees).
Look up	**Find or research by studying in a book or by looking online** *Look up* the U.S.C. on www.govinfo.gov/app/collection/uscode.
Make a living, Make ends meet	**To earn enough money to pay for expenses** The parents both worked two jobs to *make a living*. Because of the cost of living in New York City, employees must work long hours to *make ends meet*.
Make of	**Think of, consider important about** The professor asked, "What do you *make of* this case?"
Makes sense	**Is justified** It *makes sense* to study a lot, given the cost of college.
Make up	**To substitute for something that did not take place** The professor had to cancel class due to illness and therefore scheduled time to *make up* the class The professor scheduled a *makeup* class.

To invent, to create, sometimes to hide the truth
The employee decided to *make up* an excuse for missing work, rather than telling the truth that he just slept all day.

Pass away   **To die**
Justice Antonin Scalia, a famous and highly respected United States Supreme Court Justice, *passed away* suddenly during a vacation in Texas.

Pass out   **To faint, lose consciousness**
The student *passed out* after he did not eat for two days.

Side with   **Take a position consistent with**
The jury *sided with* the defendant, finding him not guilty.

The jury *sided with* the prosecution, convicting the defendant of all crimes charged.

Take a hard look   **Examine something very carefully**
The court *took a hard look* at, but ultimately rejected, the attorney's arguments.

Take a stand   **Take a position on an issue**
Protesters *took a stand* against gun violence and walked with hundreds of others across the Brooklyn Bridge.

The company *took a stand* on gun violence by refusing to sell automatic weapons.

Take the stand   **Testify in court**
In a criminal case, a defendant does not have to *take the stand* at trial.

Take-away   **Main points that one learns or should learn from a source**
What are the *take-aways* from this case; that is, what did we learn, or what does the case instruct us?

Throw out, toss   **To dismiss as in a court case**
The judge *threw out* (*tossed*) the case after deciding that the court lacked subject matter jurisdiction.

Turn down   **Reject, not grant**
The attorney applied for the job, but the employer *turned* him *down*.

The US Supreme Court *turned down* the petitioner's cert petition.

Answers to Exercises

Exercise 1: The Levels of Government

1. true (federal rules govern behavior throughout all fifty states); 2. false (California laws govern behavior within California, but Missouri is a different state, with different laws governing behavior within Missouri); 3. true; 4. false (people within one city must comply with federal laws, that city's laws, and the state laws in which the city is located; here, Tallahassee is in the state of Florida, and Georgia is a different state, with its own rules governing behavior within the state of Georgia).

Exercise 2: Governments' Powers to Create Law

Decide whether there is a valid reason for one federal government to create a uniform set of rules, whether a smaller state government should regulate the behavior in one state alone, or whether an even smaller local government should have the power to regulate the behavior of its residents. After you have read unit 2 on the legislature, you can revisit these answers.

Exercise 3: Word Fill-In

The United States has a **federal** system of government in which power is shared between a central government and the state governments. Three levels of government exist on the **federal**, **state** and **local** levels. Governments can create laws that protect people from harm, such as laws defining crimes. They can also create laws that restrict behavior, such as texting while driving, or laws that mandate (require) specific behavior, such as paying taxes.

The federal government has one uniform set of laws and can create **federal** laws affecting people throughout the United States equally. By contrast, **state** and **local** governments may have different needs and powers requiring different sets of laws that protect people within their borders. For example, states in the North with severely cold weather must have money to fund trucks, salt, and other equipment to clear snow from the roads during the winter, while states in the South must have resources to clean up following severe weather such as hurricanes.

Members of the federal government, such as the FBI and other federal law enforcement agents, may be referred to as **feds**: they protect citizens by investigating crimes. A different arm of the federal government, known as the **Fed**, is the central bank of the United States, making monetary policy, such as deciding an important interest rate.

Exercise 4: Word Forms

1. constitutional; 2. constitute (verb, "to make up"); 3. constitution (subject-noun); 4. constitutional (adjective, modifying the noun *government*); 5. constitution (object-noun); 6. constitutionally (adverb modifying the verb *to act*); 7. constitute (verb).

Exercise 5: Questions

1. Founding documents set up and define the basic rules of each level of government. Federal: Federal Constitution; state: state constitutions for each individual state; local: local founding documents such as charters. 2. There are at least fifty-one constitutions: the Federal Constitution and the fifty state constitutions. 3. It is important to distinguish between federal, state, and local founding documents because each founding document on the federal, state, and local level sets forth the rules governing how governments function and what powers each level of government has. If a level of government acts beyond those powers by taking action or enacting a form of law that is not authorized by the founding document, a court may declare that action or law (such as an executive order or a statute) of another branch unconstitutional.

Exercise 6: Questions

1. A level of government is a federal, state, or local government, and a branch of government is the specific governmental unit on all three levels: legislatures, executives, and judiciaries. 2. Branches of government on the federal level: a. Congress (federal legislature), b. federal executive (president and others), c. federal judiciary (federal courts); founding document: US (Federal) Constitution. Branches of government on the state levels: a. state legislatures, b. state executive (governors and others), c. state judiciaries (state courts); founding documents for each state: individual state constitution. Branches of government on the local levels: a. local legislatures, b. local executives (mayors and others), c. local judiciaries (local courts for local matters); founding documents for certain local counties and cities: charters.

Exercise 7: Words in Context

1. a. legislative (adjective) powers, b. executive (adjective) powers, c. judicial (adjective) powers; 2. a. Congress, b. the Senate and the House of Representatives, c. the president, d. the Supreme Court and other inferior (lower) courts, e. Congress establishes (creates) the lower federal courts.

Exercise 8: Preamble

1. a. "to form a more perfect Union" (to unify the previously divided states with one federal government), b. "to insure domestic Tranquility" (peace within the states), c.

"to provide for the common defence" (now spelled *defense*: to protect all states, especially from foreign powers), **d.** "to promote the general Welfare" (general good), **e.** to ensure liberty (freedom and fairness for all people and future generations); **2.** Future generations.

Exercise 9: Word Fill-In

1. national (referring to protecting security in the entire nation of the United States); **2.** federal; **3.** Federal, United States; **4.** feds, federal; **5.** Founding Fathers or founders or framers, federal; **6.** Fed.

Unit 1 Review

1. federal judiciary (*United States* indicates federal, and *judge* describes the judiciary); **2.** local executive (*Chicago* is a city indicating a local level, and *mayor* describes an executive); **3.** *United States* indicates federal (does not describe a branch of government); **4.** *California* indicates a state (does not describe a branch of government); **5.** federal judiciary (*United States* indicates federal, and *court* indicates judiciary); **6.** federal judiciary (*United States* indicates federal, and *court* indicates judiciary); **7.** local judiciary (*county* indicates local, and *court* indicates judiciary); **8.** local judiciary (*city* indicates local, and *court* indicates judiciary); **9.** state executive (*Iowa* indicates state, and *governor* describes an executive); **10.** federal executive (*feds* are members of the federal executive branch who carry out federal law); **11.** federal legislature (*United States* indicates federal, and *code* describes statutes from a legislature); **12.** state legislature (*New York* indicates state, and *Penal Law* is a New York State statute); **13.** federal (*national* is the federal government; does not describe a specific branch of government); **14.** state judiciary (*State of New York* indicates state, and *court* indicates judiciary); **15.** federal judiciary (*United States* indicates federal, and *court* describes the judiciary).

Exercise 10: Word Forms

1. legislators (noun); **2.** legislates (verb) (note that the verb *to legislate* means to create laws; it is therefore incorrect to state, "Congress legislates laws"; it would be correct to simply state, "Congress legislates," which alone means that Congress creates laws); **3.** congressperson (noun), Congress (noun); **4.** legislative (adjective modifying the noun *powers*), legislature (noun); **5.** legislative (adjective modifying *history*), legislators (noun), legislation (noun); **6.** congressional (adjective modifying *reports*).

Exercise 11: Constitutional Excerpts

1. every two years; **2.** every six years; **3.** representatives must be at least twenty-five years old, and senators must be at least thirty years old.

Exercise 12: Congressional Terminology

1. i; **2.** c; **3.** a; **4.** e; **5.** f or h; **6.** g; **7.** f or h; **8.** b; **9.** d.

Exercise 13: Word Fill-In

1. political gridlock; **2.** polarization; **3.** partisan.

Exercise 14: Prefixes uni-, bi-, non-

1. **bi**cameral; **2.** **Uni**ted States; **3.** **uni**cameral; **4.** **bi**partisan; **5.** **non**profit; **6.** **non**partisan; **7.** **Uni**ted States government, **uni**fy, **uni**on; **8.** **uni**form.

Exercise 15: Federal Enumerated Legislative Powers

1. U.S. Const. art. I, § 8, cl. 4; **2.** U.S. Const. art. I, § 8, cl. 8; **3.** U.S. Const. art. I, § 8, cl. 3; **4.** U.S. Const. art. I, § 8, cl. 12 (and others); **5.** U.S. Const. art. I, § 8, cl. 4; **6.** U.S. Const. art. I, § 8, cl. 8; **7.** U.S. Const. art. I, § 8, cl. 6; **8.** U.S. Const. art. I, § 8, cl. 1.

Exercise 16: The Powers of the Federal and State Governments in Context

1. Justice Roberts states that the court does not make policy and that the nation's elected leaders do that, namely, legislators in the legislature. The separation of powers gives legislative powers to Congress, not the courts. The president is also an elected leader who carries out specific policies as authorized by the Constitution and statute, within the separate powers that the Constitution allows.
2. Enumerated powers
3. Listed
4. Art. I, § 8, powers; "coin Money" (Art. I, § 8, cl. 5), "establish post Offices" (Art. I, § 8, cl. 7), and "raise and support Armies" (Art. I, § 8, cl. 12)
5. Yes. This is important because if the federal government acts beyond those powers, a person may challenge that action (executive order, proclamation, agency rule, statute) as unconstitutional.
6. Affirmative prohibitions include those in the Bill of Rights, such as restrictions on Congress in the First Amendment or in the Fourteenth Amendment on the states as well. (Research the "incorporation doctrine.")

   No, Congress does not have unfettered (unlimited) ability to pass that law: even if a law is consistent with the Bill of Rights, Congress must first have an enumerated power to enact that law, or it could be struck down or invalidated as unconstitutional.
7. States have police powers; the Tenth Amendment reserved powers.
8. See the Fourteenth Amendment, making many of the Bill of Rights amendments applicable to the states, including due process and equal protection. (Research the "incorporation doctrine.")

9. The framers wanted to ensure that the states retain these powers so that state governments, which are closer to the people in the individual states and understand the unique needs of their residents, can govern more effectively than a single federal government, which must govern uniformly throughout all of the fifty states.

Exercise 17: Words in Context

1. vest; 2. vet; 3. vet; 4. vent; 5. vests; 6. vet; 7. vet; 8. vent, vests.

Exercise 18: Words in Context

1. the commerce clause, U.S. Const. art. I, § 8, cl. 3; 2. the Committee on the Judiciary of the House of Representatives and the Committee on the Judiciary of the Senate; 3. hearing transcripts and Judiciary Committee reports from both houses of Congress.

Exercise 19: Codification of Federal Statutes

1. Title 35; 2. Title 9; 3. Title 26; 4. Title 17; 5. Title 3; 6. Title 11; 7. Title 42; 8. Title 18; 9. Title 28.

Exercise 20: The Legislative Process

1. bill; 2. a law; 3. statute; 4. act. 5. United States Code, 6. title, 7. section.

Exercise 21: Words in Context

In the early 1900s, the legislator Leonidas Dyer, a representative from the state of Missouri, introduced a **bill** in the House of Representatives to address an ever-increasing problem: car thieves were stealing motor vehicles and transporting them from one state to another in order to avoid prosecution in the state in which they stole the car. The bill received **bipartisan** support and was approved in both the House of Representatives and then the Senate. Congress **passed the law**, known by its popular name, the National Motor Vehicle Theft **Act** and the Dyer **Act** (named for Representative Dyer, the bill's sponsor). This act, when codified, became part of **Title** 18 of the United States Code. **Title** 18 of the United States Code **codifies federal** crimes.

Exercise 22: Elements of a Statute

Element #2: The firearm moved in or otherwise affected interstate or foreign commerce. **Element #3:** The individual must know or have reasonable cause to believe the place where the firearm was possessed is a school zone.

Exercise 23: Interstate and Intrastate

1. The property has been taken between two different states, transported in interstate commerce; this is a federal crime because the federal government has the power to regulate commerce; U.S. Const. art. I, § 8, cl. 3. **2.** The property has been taken from one point to another within a single state; this is a state crime.

Exercise 24: Federal, State, or Local: Who Legislates?

1. federal, 18 U.S.C. § 2312 is the current version of this statute, previously 18 U.S.C. § 408; **2.** state, as one example, N.Y. Penal Law § 155.30(8); **3.** local, as one example, Chapter 4, Title 34 of the Rules of the City of New York; **4.** all three levels of government have taxing powers allowing them to function; federal tax laws are codified in Title 26 of the U.S.C.; **5.** a state crime, as one example, N.Y. Penal Law §§ 165.00 et seq. or a federal crime if the gun moved in interstate commerce 18 U.S.C. § 922(q)(2) (A); **6.** immigration is primarily federal in nature, codified in 8 U.S.C.; 3 U.S.C. § 301 gives the president specific authority to carry out laws. States do provide some protections, as described in the preemption section, causing a conflict between federal and state law. In addition courts have adjudicated whether some state immigration laws have been preempted such as in *Arizona v. United States*, 567 U.S. 387 (2012); **7.** federal, patent laws are codified in 35 U.S.C.; **8.** federal, Patient Protection and Affordable Care Act, § 1501, Internal Revenue Code § 5000A(b), as discussed in the lesson on legislative powers. States are also involved in administering this law in accordance with this Act; **9.** state: torts are generally common law and defined by state law, but states can and have codified certain tort rules; **10.** state, as one example New York Penal Law § 155.30(3) (155.00(6) defines "secret scientific material.") **11.** local, New York City Administrative Code § 32-02(a) as authorized by a New York state statute (add the word "dogs" to an internet search to read this provision) **12.** state; contract law has common law and statutory rules. There are also federal laws governing certain provisions of contracts.

Unit 2 Review

The two houses of the federal legislature, together, are called **Congress**, which is located on **Capitol Hill** in the US **capital**, Washington, DC. The federal legislature has limited powers and can only act in accordance with the **enumerated powers** granted to it in the Constitution. One example of these limited powers is the **commerce clause**. Powers that only states have are called **reserved (or police) powers**, and those powers shared by the several levels of government are called **concurrent powers**. **Partisanship** is a noun meaning "favoring one political party," and this may cause **political gridlock** in a **polarized** Congress. This inability to **pass laws** prevents Congress from fulfilling its constitutional duty to **legislate**. If a **bill** received bipartisan support, this means that both political parties favored this measure. Congress

vets proposed legislation by holding hearings in congressional committees. If a bill passes both houses of Congress and is signed by the president it becomes a **law**, which has a specific meaning here of **statute**. Federal statutes are **codified** and printed in the official version of the statutes, called the **United States Code**. The unofficial federal code versions are the **United States Code Annotated** and the **United States Code Service**. **Elements** are specific requirements that a person must prove in case, as in the following **federal** statute. . . .

The number 18 in the citation is the **title** number of federal law and the § mark refers to the specific **section** of law.

Elements of the statute: **1.** a person knowingly aims the beam of a laser pointer; **2.** at an aircraft of at the flight path of such aircraft.

Exercise 25: Word Forms

1. executive (adjective), president (noun); **2.** presides (verb), executive (adjective); **3.** presidential (adjective); **4.** executive (noun), execute (infinitive form, *to execute* as the object of this sentence); **5.** executed (verb in the past tense)

Exercise 26: Constitutional Excerpts

1. Two-thirds of the legislators in both houses (67 in the Senate and 290 in the House) must vote to override the veto. The bill then passes without the president's approval. **2.** The bill can become a law if both houses of Congress override the president's veto or if the president does not sign it in the time prescribed in the Federal Constitution. **3.** The president did not sign the National Motor Vehicle Theft Act into law; it became a law without the president's signature because the president did not sign it or return it with his objections within the time prescribed in the Federal Constitution.

Exercise 27: Suffix -ee

1. nominee; **2.** appointee; **3.** covenantee; **4.** assignee; **5.** employee; **6.** grantee; **7.** attendees; **8.** permittee; **9.** appellee; **10.** lessee.

Exercise 28: Federal, State, or Local Executive Branch Member

1. part of the federal executive (prosecutor in federal cases); **2.** state executive; **3.** local executive; **4.** local executive (prosecutors in the city of Los Angeles); **5.** local executive (attorney representing a specific town); **6.** state executive (represents a state); **7.** federal executive (the attorney representing the United States before the US Supreme Court); **8.** federal executive (head of a federal agency); **9.** state executive (head of a state agency); **10.** local executive (New York City agency).

Unit 3 Review

Article II of the United States Constitution establishes the largest of the three federal branches of government, the **executive** branch of government, employing over four million people. The president heads this branch, which **executes**, enforces or carries out, the laws. One way that the president carries out the laws is by appointing the Cabinet members, including the heads of agencies, called secretaries, the attorney general, and United States attorneys in the different federal districts. US attorneys prosecute criminal cases in the federal courts and defend the government in civil cases. The president can issue **executive** orders and can direct agencies to carry out the law.

Administrative agencies are part of the **executive** branch. Agency members may have specialized knowledge of specific subject areas in order to effectively **execute** (carry out) laws as authorized by Congress, such as regulations from certain administrative agencies including the Food and Drug Administration (FDA). Congress must affirmatively grant an agency the power to **promulgate** regulations.

Exercise 29: Word Forms

1. vests, judicial, judiciary; 2. vet, justices, judicial; 3. judiciary, vests; 4. adjudicate; 5. adjudged; 6. judge.

Exercise 30: Civil or Criminal Case?

1. CR, S (defendants are prosecuted in criminal cases; they are sued in civil cases; here "N.Y. Penal Law" is a state law, prosecuted in state court); 2. CI, S/F (libel is a type of civil action for making false statements, and a party may sue in a state or, if a federal court has subject matter jurisdiction, in a federal court); 3. CR, S/F (there is a burden of proof in both civil and criminal cases, but the term *prosecution* indicates that this is a criminal case; parties *file suit* or *bring suit* in a civil case); 4. CI/CR, S/F (experts may testify in both civil and criminal cases in all levels of courts); 5. CI, S/F (contract actions are civil actions and may be brought in state court and in a federal if the federal court has subject matter jurisdiction); 6. CI, S/F (*liable* means civilly responsible; *guilty* means criminally responsible in all levels of court); 7. CR, S/F (*not guilty* means a person was found not responsible in a criminal case; synonym is *to acquit*, in all levels of court); 8. CR, S (the district attorney prosecutes criminal cases in violation of state law; N.Y. Vehicle and Traffic Law is a New York state law); 9. CR, F (18 U.S.C. contains the federal crimes prosecuted in federal courts); 10. CI/CR, S/F (a psychologist could testify in a criminal or civil case in all levels of court); 11. CI, F (*brought suit* signifies starting a civil suit; *United States* is a synonym for *federal* here, so this is a federal court); 12. CI, S/F (a jury may award damages, or monetary compensation, in civil cases); 13. CI, S/F (in civil cases, parties may choose to settle before a jury reaches a verdict;. 14. CR, S/F (in criminal cases, a defendant may

choose to take a plea, or agree to certain charges, to avoid going to trial and possibly face a longer sentence); **15.** CI/CR, S/F (judges charge, or instruct the jury, in both civil and criminal cases in all levels of court); **16.** CI/CR, S/F (witnesses testify, or take the stand, in both civil and criminal cases in all levels of court); **17.** CI/CR, S (civil and criminal trials take place in a trial court; here the Supreme Court likely refers to a New York State trial court, not the United States Supreme Court; if the US Supreme Court has original jurisdiction, this could be F as well); **18.** CI, S/F (*damages* means monetary compensation in civil cases; these can be awarded both state and federal courts).

Exercise 31: Selected "People" in a Court Case

1. p; **2.** s; **3.** o; **4.** k; **5.** j; **6.** i; **7.** q; **8.** r; **9.** f; **10.** d; **11.** n; **12.** g; **13.** b; **14.** h; **15.** c; **16.** a; **17.** e; **18.** l; **19.** m.

Exercise 32: The Judiciary and Related Terminology

1. false (Article III judges are named so for the US Constitution, Article III, establishing the federal judiciary); **2.** true; **3.** true (the trial judge only charges or instructs the jury; a party can appeal and claim that the judge improperly charged [gave incorrect instructions to] the jurors, and the appellate court would review the trial judge's jury charge; but only the trial court judge gives the instructions to the jurors); **4.** true; **5.** false (trials take place in trial courts, and higher courts review the lower trial court decisions); **6.** false (witnesses testify in trial courts; an appellate court can review the record [written transcripts of the witness testimony at the trial, exhibits] from the trial to determine if there was any reversible error, such as the trial judge allowing a witness to give testimony over an attorney's objection [sustaining an objection], which resulted in reversible error); **7.** true; **8.** true; **9.** true; **10.** false (only one judge presides at a trial); **11.** false (there are nine justices; a majority is five); **12.** false (juries only hear testimony in trial courts during jury [but not bench] trials); **13.** true; **14.** true; **15.** true (a plaintiff who won and does not appeal is the appellee if the defendant appeals); **16.** true (a defendant who loses at trial can appeal and is the appellant on appeal); **17.** true (*petitioner*), false (*defendant*) (when a party files a petition for a writ of injunction or a writ of habeas corpus, the parties are called *petitioner* and *respondent*); **18.** false (a prosecutor is a party in a criminal case, and a lawsuit only refers to a civil case).

Exercise 33: Federal District Courts

1. United States District Court for the District of Rhode Island; **2.** United States District Court for the Northern District of California, United States District Court for the Eastern District of California, United States District Court for the Central District of California, and United States District Court for the Southern District of

California; **3.** United States District Court for the Northern District of Texas, United States District Court for the Southern District of Texas, United States District Court for the Western District of Texas, and United States District Court for the Eastern District of Texas; **4.** United States District Court for the Northern District of Florida, United States District Court for the Middle District of Florida, and United States District Court for the Southern District of Florida; **5.** United States District Court for the District of Idaho; **6.** United States District Court for the Western District of Washington and United States District Court for the Eastern District of Washington; **7.** United States District Court for the District of North Dakota.

Exercise 34: Appeals to the Circuit Courts

1. Fifth Circuit Court of Appeals; **2.** Ninth Circuit Court of Appeals; **3.** Tenth Circuit Court of Appeals; **4.** Second Circuit Court of Appeals; **5.** Ninth Circuit Court of Appeals; **6.** First Circuit Court of Appeals; **7.** the United States Supreme Court; **8.** the United States Supreme Court; **9.** the United States Supreme Court; **10.** there is no further appeal possible; this is the high court, the federal court of last resort; **11.** the United States Supreme Court.

Exercise 35: Which Federal Court?

1. the United States Supreme Court; **2.** the United States Supreme Court; **3.** a federal appeals court; **4.** a federal trial court; **5.** a federal appeals court; **6.** a federal trial court; **7.** the United States Supreme Court; **8.** the United States Supreme Court; **9.** a federal appeals court; **10.** the United States Supreme Court.

Exercise 36: US Supreme Court Review

1. discretionary; means that the court has discretion or choice in picking cases for review; **2.** federal (*United States* is a synonym); circuit courts of appeals; **3.** the highest court of any of the states; **4.** the highest state courts and the intermediate courts in the federal system, called *circuit courts* or *US courts of appeals*.

Exercise 37: Transparent or Opaque

1. opaque; **2.** opaque; **3.** transparent; **4.** opaque; **5.** transparent; **6.** opaque; **7.** opaque.

Exercise 38: Certiorari and Transparency

Case 1: 1. Justice Stevens; **2.** yes, the court was transparent and open by stating the reason for granting cert; **3.** the court tackled the difficult issue of the amount of punitive damages that the Constitution would allow, i.e., what is a constitutional measure for awarding punitive damages. **Case 2: 1.** Justice Holmes; **2.** this is a federal crime, which we know because of the citation, 18 U.S.C., which codifies federal crimes; **3.** yes, the court was transparent when it stated that it would decide if an aircraft was included in a federal statute, the National Motor Vehicle Theft Act, although the court did not explain why it would decide this issue; **4.** no, the US Supreme Court reversed and did not agree with the lower court; **5.** no, it did not let the decision stand (leave it as it was); it reversed. **Case 3: 1.** Chief Justice Warren; **2.** *Vignera v. New York* came from a state court, from New York's top court, the New York Court of Appeals; *Westover v United States* came from a federal court, the US Court of Appeals for the Ninth Circuit; *California v. Stewart* came from a state court, California's high court, the Supreme Court of California; **3.** yes, the court was transparent and open by stating the reason for granting cert; **4.** it was important to give clear guidance to law enforcement about how to protect individuals' federal constitutional rights when being interrogated by law enforcement. **Case 4: 1.** this case originated in a federal court, as seen from the fact that it was appealed to the Fourth Circuit Court of Appeals; **2.** yes, the court was transparent and open by stating the reason for granting cert; **3.** the citation "42 U.S.C. § 1988" informs the reader that this is a federal statute (U.S.C.) in Title 42 on the subject of The Public Health and Welfare; **4.** the court cites precedents from the Eighth Circuit Court of Appeals (CA 8), from the Eleventh Circuit Court of Appeals (CA 11), and one decision from the Third Circuit Court of Appeals (CA 3) to show that there was a circuit conflict; the Fourth Circuit decision on this issue was different from the Eighth Circuit, Eleventh Circuit, and Third Circuit decisions; **5.** "to resolve a Circuit conflict" between the lower circuit courts, often referred to as a "split among the circuits." **Case 5: 1.** Chief Justice Rehnquist wrote this opinion; **2.** yes, the court was transparent and open by stating the reason for granting cert; **3.** the court took on (granted cert and agreed to hear the case) because this was "an important issue." **Case 6: 1.** no, this is not a decision on the merits of the case, only on the denial of a petition for a writ of certiorari, refusing to hear the case; **2.** no, the court was opaque; it did not explain why it denied cert; **3.** no, the court did not rule on the issue; it denied cert, refusing to hear the case.

Exercise 39: Criminal Cases

1. "18 U.S.C." informs the reader that this is a federal criminal statute because it means *Title 18 of the United States Code*, on the subject of federal crimes and criminal procedure; **2.** "district courts of the United States" means federal trial courts; **3.** "original jurisdiction" means, in this context, where the case originates or begins, here, a federal trial court; **3.** "exclusive" here means to exclude, and states cannot adjudicate federal crimes (the trials for federal crimes take place exclusively in federal courts); **4.** "offenses against the laws of the United States" means federal laws (United States).

Exercise 40: Written Decisions and Level of Court

1. This is not a written decision of a judge but the actual case being tried in a federal trial court, a US district court. **2.** This is a written decision of a judge, federal trial court (the *Federal Supplement* prints federal trial court decisions in books called *reporters*). **3.** This is a written decision of a judge, from the federal appeals court (*Federal Reporters* print federal appeals court decisions in books called *reporters*). **4.** This is a written decision of a judge. The *United States Reports* (*U.S.*) is a reporter, a book, that prints US Supreme Court decisions. **5.** This is not a written decision of a judge. This is the judge's belief or opinion. The court is not apparent. **6.** This is not a written decision of a judge. This is what the judge decided to do, but there is no reference to any form of a writing. If this sentence stated that "the judge's decision is printed in a reporter," then that statement refers to a written decision, illustrating where the decision is printed. The court is not apparent. **7.** This is a written decision of a judge. The court is not apparent.

Exercise 41: Describing the Vote of the Appellate Courts

1. adjective (modifying *opinion*); **2.** verb; **3.** noun; **4.** verb; **5.** adjective (modifying *opinion*); **6.** adjective (modifying *opinion*); **7.** verb; **8.** noun.

Exercise 42: Short Opinion from the US Supreme Court

1. The parties are the United States of America and the State of Texas. The United States, listed first, is the petitioner and filed the cert petition. **2.** The case originated in a federal court, as the appeal came from the United States Court of Appeals for the Fifth Circuit. **3.** There is no named author; this is a per curiam opinion. **4.** Four justices agreed, and four justices disagreed. When there is a tie, the lower court decision stands, and the Supreme Court affirmed the lower court due to the 4–4 tie. **5.** The court's vote was "equally divided" because one judge did not take part in the decision. Only eight justices heard the case.

Exercise 43: Federal, State, or Local: Who Adjudicates?

Use the suggested internet search to find the answers.

Unit 4 Review

Article III of the United States Constitution establishes the federal **judiciary**, consisting of the federal courts. During a civil lawsuit or a criminal prosecution, a **judge** interprets the law on a case-by-case basis.

18 U.S.C. § 2312 **proscribes** knowingly transporting a stolen "motor vehicle" in interstate commerce. A defendant who is charged with stealing and transporting an inoperable car across state lines could claim that an inoperable car is not a "motor vehicle." The court would interpret § 2312 and the definition of "motor vehicle," which 18 U.S.C. § 2311 **prescribes**, in order to decide whether an inoperable car is a "motor vehicle." Because 18 U.S.C. § 2312 is a federal criminal statute, the **litigation**

would take place in a federal court; the attorneys would **litigate** the case, and the judge would **adjudicate** the legal issues in the case.

Courts can also decide if a statute is inconsistent with one or more provisions of the Constitution. In *Marbury v. Madison*, 5 U.S. 137 (1803), the United States Supreme Court first articulated the principle that the judiciary has the ultimate responsibility to review and invalidate unconstitutional statutes. **Judicial** review is an important power of the **judiciary** in the US system of checks and balances.

Common law consists of rules that evolve through court decisions, and statutory law is enacted by legislatures.

Unit 5 Review

Look up the cases on the internet or a research platform to find the answers.

Notes

Unit 1. Overview of the Government in the United States

1. White House, "Our Government: State and Local Government," www.whitehouse.gov.
2. The New York Constitution's home rule provisions provide that local governments only have the power to create local laws regarding issues of "property, affairs or government." Gerald Benjamin, *Home Rule: Elusive or Illusion?*, 89 N.Y.S. Bar J. 25, 27 (Oct. 2017) (quoting N.Y. Constitution in force in 1938, Article XII, § 4). In fact, the New York State Legislature in Albany passes many laws affecting issues of a seemingly local nature in cities throughout New York. The New York State Constitution and statutes create the entire system of state courts, including local courts that hear cases arising only within one city, village, or county.
3. Local legislative bodies are limited in their power to enact local laws. Gerald Benjamin, "Home Rule: Elusive or Illusion?," *New York State Bar Journal* 89 (October 2017): 25.
4. United States Senate, "Constitution of the United States," www.senate.gov.

Unit 2. The Federal Legislature

1. United States Senate, "Dates and Sessions of Congress," www.senate.gov.
2. United States Senate, "Political Parties," www.senate.gov.
3. *Merriam-Webster Dictionary*, s.v. "partisan," www.merriam-webster.com.
4. *National Federation of Independent Business v. Sebelius*, 567 U.S. 519, 534 (2012).
5. Patient Protection and Affordable Care Act, § 1501, Internal Revenue Code § 5000A(b).
6. The government also unsuccessfully claimed that the "necessary and proper clause" in Article I, § 8, gave Congress the power to enact this law.
7. The Bill of Rights refers to the first ten amendments to the Federal Constitution. One example of an affirmative prohibition in the Bill of Rights is the First Amendment, which states in part, "Congress shall make no law abridging the freedom of speech." U.S. Const. amend. I.
8. For a detailed discussion of preemption in the field of marijuana regulation, see Erwin Chemerinsky, Jolene Forman, Allen Hopper, and Sam Kamin, "Cooperative Federalism and Marijuana Possession," *UCLA Law Review* 62 (2015): 74–122; and Erwin Chemerinsky, "Introduction: Marijuana Laws and Federalism," *Boston College Law Review* 58 (2017): 857–62.
9. Chemerinsky et al., "Cooperative Federalism," 77.
10. See Giffords Law Center to Prevent Gun Violence, "Preemption of Local Laws," 2017, http://lawcenter.giffords.org. The US Constitution does, however, restrict both federal and state regulation.
11. Giffords Law Center.
12. See United States Senate, "Supreme Court Nomination Hearings," www.senate.gov.

13. For a list of the many congressional committees, see the United State Senate and United States House of Representatives websites.
14. *Plain meaning* is a statutory construction rule, which is a type of rule that governs how courts interpret statutes.
15. See, e.g., Antonin Scalia and Bryan A. Garner, *Reading Law: The Interpretation of Legal Texts* (Eagan, MN: Thomson West, 2012).
16. Under Article II, Section 2, of the US Constitution, the president nominates US Supreme Court judicial candidates, who are approved (after hearings) with the "advice and consent of the Senate."
17. The law prohibiting the possession of a gun with 1,000 feet of a school zone is formally called the Gun Free School Zones *Act*. The set of laws that together govern whether a United States citizen has to purchase health care is called the Patient Protection and Affordable Care *Act*. The Office of the Law Revision Council of the United States House of Representatives defines the term *Act* as "a bill or joint resolution that has passed both the US House of Representatives and Senate and has been signed into law by the President, or passed over the President's veto, thus becoming a law." Office of the Law Revision Counsel, United States Code, "Detailed Guide to the United States Code Content and Features," http://uscode.house.gov.
18. US Government Printing Office, "United States Code," www.govinfo.gov.
19. The term *elements* is also used to describe what a person must prove for other types of rules, such as common law rules in civil cases. Usually, the plaintiff, or the person bringing the lawsuit, must prove (produce evidence through witness testimony or other evidence such as a business records, a contract, or even emails) to win the case. In a criminal case, the government, and not the person accused of a crime, has the burden of proving the defendant's guilt.
20. See Congressional Research Service (CRS), Reports for Congress, *How Bills Amend Statutes*, RS20617, June 24, 2008, www.everycrsreport.com.
21. The Affordable Care Act: the Patient Protection Patient Protection and Affordable Care Act and the Health Care and Education Reconciliation Act of 2010.

Unit 3. The Federal Executive

1. White House, "Our Government: The Executive Branch," www.whitehouse.gov. This informative website also gives detailed descriptions on the structure and function of the executive branch.
2. White House.
3. For a list of executive departments, subagencies, and independent agencies, see USA.gov, "Branches of the U.S. Government," www.usa.gov.
4. Department of Homeland Security, "Topics," www.dhs.gov.
5. Proclamations "communicate[] information on holidays, commemorations, special observances, trade and policy." Federal Register, "Proclamations," www.federalregister.gov.
6. History, "This Day in History, Oct. 3, 1863," www.history.com.
7. Proclamation No. 9645, 82 Fed. Reg. 45161 (Sept. 24, 2017).
8. Aaron Blake, "What Is an Executive Order? And How Do President Trump's Stack Up?," *Washington Post*, January 27, 2017, www.washingtonpost.com.
9. Steven Rattner, "Pushing Obamacare over the Cliff," *New York Times*, March 28, 2017, www.nytimes.com.

10. Exec. Order 13765, 82 Fed. Reg. 8351 (2017).

11. Exec. Order No. 13769, 82 Fed. Reg. 8977 (2017); and Exec. Order No.13780, 82 Fed. Reg. 13209 (2017).

12. Mireya Navarro, "Federal Housing Officials Warn against Blanket Bans of Ex-Offenders," *New York Times*, April 4, 2016, A14. "Federal officials said landlords must distinguish between arrests and convictions and cannot use an arrest to *ban* applicants."

13. 790.065(13), Fla. Stat. (2018).

14. US Department of Health and Human Services, "Laws & Regulations," www.hhs.gov.

15. The rulemaking process and publication requirements are very specific. For an overview, see Office of the Federal Register, "A Guide to the Rulemaking Process," 2011, www.federal register.gov.

16. *National Federation of Independent Business v. Sebelius*, 567 U.S. 519 (2012).

17. Andrew Couts, "Emerging Tech: Can Amazon's Prime Air Drones Take Off Covered in All This Red Tape?," *Digital Trends*, December 3, 2013, www.digitaltrends.com.

18. In the 113th Congress, there was a Republican majority in the House of Representatives, a Democratic majority in the Senate, and a Democratic president, President Obama. Partisanship resulted in Congress's failure to pass certain Democratic initiatives. President Obama used his executive powers to "carry out key elements" regulating certain areas without congressional approval, such as "raising the minimum wage for employees of federal contractors, and allowing the Environmental Protection Agency to curb carbon emissions from coal plants," which Republicans viewed as executive overreach. Ashley Parker, "Boehner to Seek Bill to Sue Obama over Executive Actions," *New York Times*, June 25, 2014, A16.

19. The US president nominates and, when confirmed, appoints only the lead US attorney in the federal districts but not the assistant US attorneys (AUSAs). Similarly, on the state and local levels, only the lead state attorney general and the local district attorneys are either elected or appointed and not the assistants (attorneys) who work for them.

Unit 4. The Federal Judiciary

1. U.S. Const. art. III, §1.

2. Administrative Office of the US Courts, "Table 4.10: U.S. District Courts—Civil Cases Terminated, by Action Taken, during the 12-Month Periods Ending June 30, 1990, and September 30, 1995 through 2017" and "Table 5.4: U.S. District Courts—Criminal Defendants Disposed of, by Method of Disposition, during the 12-Month Periods Ending June 30, 1990, and September 30, 1995 through 2017," Judicial Facts and Figures, www.uscourts.gov.

3. Administrative Office of the US Courts, "Criminal Cases," www.uscourts.gov.

4. Federal Judicial Center, *Guide to Research in Federal Judicial History* (Washington, DC: Federal Judicial Center, Federal Judicial History Office, 2010), 85, www.fjc.gov.

5. Administrative Office of the US Courts, "Court Role and Structure," www.uscourts.gov.

6. There are situations when the prosecution can appeal, such as when a judge suppresses (keeps out) evidence at trial, but not when a jury finds the defendant not guilty.

7. Supreme Court of the United States, "FAQs—Supreme Court Justices," www.supremecourt.gov.

8. If a party does choose to appeal, there is much work involved in completing an appeal.

9. There are exceptions. Appellate courts have specific rules on what types of issues they will review and when there is an appeal as of right.

10. Supreme Court of the United States, "FAQs—General Information," www.supremecourt.gov.
11. Bryan A. Garner, ed., *Black's Law Dictionary*, 10th ed. (Eagan, MN: Thomson Reuters, 2014), s.v. "standing," quoting *Baker v. Carr*, 369 U.S. 186, 204 (1962).
12. *Harrington v. Richter*, 562 U.S. 86, 99 (2011).
13. Supreme Court of the United States, *Rules of the Supreme Court of the United States*, effective November 13, 2017, 5–6, www.supremecourt.gov. *Local rules* of courts govern practice before a court, including the duties of attorneys appearing before the court, how documents are filed, and the required format of certain papers, such as motion papers and many others. Each court lists its rules on the court's website.
14. Amanda Reilly, "Water Policy," *E&E News*, July 23, 2018, www.eenews.net.
15. Vince Sullivan, *Law360* (blog), May 18, 2018, www.law360.com.
16. Adam Liptak, *New York Times*, December 5, 2008, www.nytimes.com.
17. Bill Donahue, *Law360* (blog), June 28, 2018, www.law360.com (the high court chose to address an issue because some circuit courts of appeals reached a different conclusion from other circuit courts of appeals, called a *split* among the circuits).
18. Bryan Garner, "Law Prose Lesson #165, 'Ruling' vs. 'Opinion' vs. 'Judgment,' Etc.," *Law Prose* (blog), May 27, 2015, www.lawprose.org.
19. Richard Wolf, *USA Today*, May 27, 2014, www.usatoday.com.
20. Ariane de Vogue, *CNN Politics*, November 29, 2017, www.cnn.com.
21. Adam Liptak, *New York Times*, June 23, 2015, at B2.
22. Fran Spielman, *Chicago Sun Times*, April 24, 2017, http://chicago.suntimes.com.
23. Joe Palazzolo, *Wall Street Journal*, June 20, 2016, www.wsj.com.
24. Mark Sherman, Associated Press, June 15, 2018, https://apnews.com.
25. Federal circuit courts issuing contrary decisions interpreting the same provision of law is called a *split among the circuits*.
26. *Davis v. Passman*, 442 U.S. 228, 239 n. 18 (1979) (citations omitted). There are a number of other reasons why courts may or may not hear a case including the following. The concept of *justiciability* relates to there being a *case or controversy* as Article III of the US Constitution requires and includes concepts, with varying rules, such as *standing*, *mootness*, and *ripeness*. In addition, there are detailed rules governing when a court can exercise personal jurisdiction over certain defendants.
27. James W. Moore, *Moore's Federal Practice*, 3rd ed. (New York: Matthew Bender, 2018), 17A, § 120.12.
28. New York State Unified Court System, "Courts outside New York City Overview," www.nycourts.gov.
29. Bryan A. Garner, ed., *Black's Law Dictionary*, 10th ed. (Eagan, MN: Thomson Reuters, 2014), 293.
30. When citing a specific portion of a case (by quoting from or otherwise referring to any part of the opinion), legal writers also indicate the exact page(s) on which the quotation or other reference appears. This is called a *pinpoint (pin) cite* or a *jump cite*. For example, if a legal writer were quoting a sentence from page 26 of *McBoyle v. United States*, the citation would appear as *McBoyle v. United States*, 283 U.S. 25, 26 (1931), if the quotation is given the first time the case is cited. The "26" is the pinpoint cite, pinpointing the exact location of the reference in the cited source. Citation manuals such as *The Bluebook: A Uniform System of Citation*, ed. Columbia Law Review Association et al., 20th ed. (2015) and jurisdiction-specific style manuals contain other rules for citing authorities.

31. Citation rules vary depending on the style book. Individual states have their own style manuals, and it is essential to know which style manual to follow. See, e.g., Edward W. Jessen, *California Style Manual*, 4th ed. (San Francisco: West Group, 2000).

32. *Merriam-Webster Dictionary*, s.v. "progeny," www.merriam-webster.com.

33. However, after a jury renders a verdict, an attorney may make what is called a *posttrial motion*, requesting that the judge set aside the jury verdict, often claiming that the evidence was not sufficient. The judge may write a decision explaining why he or she granted or denied the attorney's motion.

34. Benjamin N. Cardozo, *The Nature of the Judicial Process* (New Haven, CT: Yale University Press, 1921), 13.

35. Linda Edwards, *Legal Writing and Analysis*, 4th ed. (New York: Wolters Kluwer, 2015), 33–34.

36. Edwards, 33–34.

37. Consult a good legal-writing text, such as Linda Edwards's book *Legal Writing and Analysis*, to identify the different rule structures. Elements are just one type of rule structure.

38. *McDougall v. Lamm*, 211 N.J. 203, 214–15 (2012) (quoting *Portee v. Jaffee*, 84 N.J. 88, 101 (1980)).

39. *Id.*

40. *Id.*

41. *Id.*

42. *Id.* at 219–20.

43. *Id.* at 221–22.

44. Courts may choose to rely on precedents that are not binding on them, such as decisions from different states. Courts must follow precedent that is binding, such as decisions in courts that are in their direct line of appeal. There are many rules governing when precedents are either binding or persuasive, and these rules may even vary by jurisdiction.

45. Joanna Sugden, *Wall Street Journal*, June 12, 2018, A8.

46. Michael C. Bender, Michael R. Gordon, and Jonathan Cheng, "Trump, Kim Start Summit Talks," *Wall Street Journal*, June 12, 2018, A1, A9.

47. Steven M. Witzel and Joshua D. Roth, "Implications of the DOJ and Apple Legal Fight That Wasn't," *New York Law Journal*, May 5, 2016, 9, quoting Apple, "A Message to Our Customers," February 16, 2016, available at www.apple.com/customer-letter/.

48. Bryan Garner, "Law Prose Lesson #165, 'Ruling' vs. 'Opinion' vs. 'Judgment, Etc.'," *Law Prose* (blog), May 27, 2015, www.lawprose.org.

49. In federal courts, the Federal Rules of Evidence govern the admissibility of evidence.

50. When a later court *overrules* a different, earlier decision, the result in that earlier case does not *automatically* change; i.e., cases decided after *Betts* and before *Gideon* are not *automatically reversed* just because *Gideon overruled Betts*. But they may change if a court finds that the new rule is *retroactive*, that is, applies to cases decided before *Gideon*.

51. Roy L. Reardon and William T. Russell Jr., "Overturning Precedent on Meaning of Parenting," *New York Law Journal*, October 19, 2016, 3.

Unit 5. Separation of Powers and Checks and Balances

1. Thomas R. Newman and Steven J. Ahmuty Jr., "Urging a Change in the Law: When to Set Aside Precedent?," *New York Law Journal*, May 6, 2015, 3.

2. *Brown v. Board of Education*, 347 U.S. 483 (1954), overruling the principle of "separate but equal" in the context of education for people of different races.

3. Newman and Ahmuty, "Urging a Change," 3, citing *People v. Bing*, 76 N.Y.2d 331, 337–38 (1990), quoting *Danann Realty v. Harris*, 5 N.Y.2d 317, 322 (1959).

4. Newman and Ahmuty, 3, citing *People v. Hobson*, 39 N.Y.2d 479, 489 (1976), *Illinois Brick Co. v. Illinois*, 431 U.S. 720, 736 (1977).

5. *National Federation of Independent Business v. Sebelius*, 567 U.S. 519, 537–38 (2012).

6. *Id.*

7. The Affordable Care Act consists of the Patient Protection Patient Protection and Affordable Care Act and the Health Care and Education Reconciliation Act of 2010 and is known colloquially as "Obamacare."

8. There were other issues and other votes of the court in this case, not discussed here.

9. "The term 'school zone' means—(A) in, or on the grounds of, a public, parochial or private school; or (B) within a distance of 1,000 feet from the grounds of a public, parochial or private school." 18 U.S.C. § 921(a)(25).

10. Newman and Ahmuty, "Urging a Change," 3.

11. Proclamation No. 9645, 82 Fed. Reg. 45161 (Sept. 24, 2017).

12. *Trump v. Hawaii*, 585 U.S. ___, 138 S. Ct. 2392, 2403 (2018).

13. To read the proclamation in its entirety, see www.whitehouse.gov.

14. Newman and Ahmuty, 3, quoting *Matter of Eckhardt*, 39 N.Y.2d 493, 499 (1976).

15. Newman and Ahmuty, 3, quoting *Eckhardt*, 39 N.Y.2d at 499, *Woods v. Lancet*, 303 N.Y.349, 354 (1951).

16. *McDougall v. Lamm*, 211 N.J. 203, 220–21 (2012).

17. New York Lab. Law § 202-k (McKinney 2015).

Illustration Credits

Page

1   *Federal Constitution:* Public domain; Constitutional Convention, 1789, from National Archives / Wikimedia Commons, https://commons.wikimedia.org/wiki/File:United_States_Constitution.jpg.

3   *Map of the United States:* blambca/Shutterstock.com.

4   *Map of the separate US states:* Sjgh/Shutterstock.com.

4   *Map of New York counties:* Public domain; ZooFari / Wikimedia Commons, 28 September 2010, https://commons.wikimedia.org/wiki/File:Map_of_New_York_counties.svg.

8   *FBI, the feds:* Pamela Au/Shutterstock.com.

8   *The Fed:* Tanarch/Shutterstock.com.

10 *Federal Constitution:* Public domain; Constitutional Convention, 1789, from National Archives / Wikimedia Commons, https://commons.wikimedia.org/wiki/File:United_States_Constitution.jpg.

11 *New York State Constitution:* Public domain; transcribed from New York State Constitution excerpts, www.dos.ny.gov/info/pdfs/Constitution.pdf.

11 *New York City Charter:* Public domain; transcribed from New York City Charter excerpts, http://www.nyc.gov/html/records/pdf/section%201133_citycharter.pdf; State of New York Legislative Bill Drafting Commission.

19 *Silos:* Graphic stocker/Shutterstock.com.

22 *Thurgood Marshall United States Courthouse:* Photo by the author; © 2015 Karen M. Ross. All rights reserved.

27 *Capitol:* Photo by the author; © 2010 Karen M. Ross. All rights reserved.

29 *Capitol, wide view:* fstockfoto/Shutterstock.com.

33 *Congressional floor:* Rob Crandall/Shutterstock.com.

35 *Donkey:* Coprid/Shutterstock.com.

35 *Elephant:* Gualtiero boffi/Shutterstock.com.

36 *Map of the US illustrating red, blue, and purple states:* Public domain; Zhorken / Wikimedia Commons, 25 May 2008, https://commons.wikimedia.org/wiki/File:2008PresMap.svg.

37 *Gridlock:* Trial/Shutterstock.com.

38 *Globe:* Mapichai/Shutterstock.com.

39 *Congressional aisle:* Drop of Light/Shutterstock.com.

40 *Unicycle:* aliaksei kruhlenia/Shutterstock.com.

40 *Bicycle:* stockphoto-graf/Shutterstock.com.

53 *House of Representatives report:* Public domain; transcribed from H.R. Rep. No. 66-312 (1919) excerpts.

54 *Helen Keller statue:* Photo by the author, in Emancipation Hall, US Capitol Visitor Center, Washington, DC; Helen Keller sculpture © 2009 Edward Hlavka; photograph © 2010 Karen M. Ross. All rights reserved.

Index

About the Author

Karen Ross is Director of the Legal English Program at New York University School of Law and is a member of the Graduate Lawyering Program faculty. She holds a master's degree in teaching English to speakers of other languages and a Juris Doctor degree, and she has taught legal English to hundreds of international lawyers.